D1558482

Factory Decoys
of Mason, Stevens, Dodge, and Peterson

by John and Shirley Delph

Schiffer Publishing Ltd

Box E, Exton, Pennsylvania 19341

Acknowledgements

Jim Aikin, Dick Clark, Jim Cook, Bernard Crandell, Robert Creighton, William Crooks, Michael Delph, Ed Denavarre, Bernard Giacoletto, Gene Gissin, Alan Haid, Lowell Jackson, Frank Klay, John Lellos, Roger Ludwig, Dick Meder, John Mulak, Al Nyberg, John Owen, Bruce Randolph, Randy Root, Ray Schalk, Jerry St. John, Shelburne Museum, George Thompson, Joe Tonelli, Bob Vigaletti, Howard Waddell.

Book Design: Steven Carothers

Library of Congress Catalog Card Number: 80–52025
ISBN 0-916838-33-1

Printed in the United States of America
Schiffer Publishing Limited, Box E, Exton, Pa. 19341

Dedication

To Michael—
> for all the hours spent rummaging through antique shops and shows, visiting museums, and waiting while we talked "shop" with other collectors. Our indispensible scout and now a second generation collector.

(1) How's this for a hunting rig?

TABLE OF CONTENTS

An anonymous collection of rare masons.

Introduction

Who would have thought that a purchase at an antique show in a small New England church would lead to our writing a book on decoys? Not us, certainly!! This first "find" whetted our appetite for decoys and our appetite has grown voraciously ever since. Unfortunately, our pocketbook has a hard time keeping up with it. A common problem with us all!

Mason decoys, through a quirk of fate, became our specialty. Living in Pennsylvania at the time, we were on one of our frequent pilgrimages to New England in search of painted furniture and accessories. We were wandering around the booths of the antique show when a decoy caught our attention. Our knowledge of decoys was nil then, but it just seemed to say "buy me." (It later turned out to be a "Detroit" Grade Canvas Back Drake in super condition.) After the usual haggling about price, we settled on forty dollars. Not aware that it was a Mason, we left content in the knowledge that it would look good among our painted things.

On our way home we stopped at an antique shop and were surprised to find another decoy that looked very similar to the one we'd just bought. It had the same body style but a different paint pattern. The owner said, "Oh, yeah. That's a Mason Mallard Drake. The price is sixty dollars." Sold! Here we had spent one hundred dollars and didn't know a Mason from a Stevens. We just hoped we hadn't blown our money.

Upon arriving home, we scoured our personal and local library and bookstores. The lack of reference material was disheartening. Through other collectors we met, we were able to beg, borrow, and buy decoy books. As we became more serious collectors, our decoy library grew and is now quite complete; yet, we felt the need for a reference book on factory birds. This led to this book which we hope will help the beginning collector, the antique dealer who finds decoys occasionally, and the advanced collector.

It seemed the more we learned, the more we wanted to know. Luckily, the decoy has become an integral part of the folk art market, and more is being written about them all the time. As a part of our sporting heritage, the decoy's popularity, as well as its value, has steadily increased during the last decade. This interest has rescued innumerable birds from barns, attics, and boat sheds. What might have been reduced to ashes or relegated to the dump is now preserved for future generations of collectors.

It's impossible to fully understand the use of decoys in waterfowl hunting without considering the important role of factory birds. Adele Earnest, in her book, The Art of the Decoy: American Bird Carvings, chronicles the evolution of the decoy in exquisite detail. No attempt will be made to duplicate that here, but we will try to put the role of factory birds in perspective.

Market hunters, men who killed waterfowl in large numbers for profit, flourished during the late 19th and early 20th Century. Wildfowl, such as ducks, geese, and shorebirds, were sold by the barrelful to wholesale food markets in large cities across the country. The advent of the double-barreled shotgun brought with it an open invitation for slaughter. Scores of ducks fell before a single gunner daily, keeping restaurateurs well-stocked and patrons happy. This carnage continued until 1913 when all night shooting, spring shooting, and shipment of birds was outlawed by a federal migratory bird act. Legal market hunting ground to a halt in 1918 when the United States and Canada enacted the Migratory Bird Treaty Act. The shooting of shorebirds and hunting with "tollers" or live decoys also became illegal and the conservation of wildlife became the responsibility of the federal and state governments.

Large numbers of decoys were indispensible to the market hunters and the manufacturers of factory decoys met this need by providing good hunting birds at reasonable prices. Hundreds of sporting hunters found these decoys well-suited to their needs, especially those without the talent or inclination for hand-carving their own rig. The result was a business relationship mutually beneficial to both hunter and manufacturer.

Although there were tens of small "factories" over the years, we've limited this book to our four favorites, Mason, Stevens, Dodge, and Peterson. Chronologically, the order is reversed. It's difficult to give exact dates for their inception because they're not known, but they did span the period from 1873 to 1924. We do know that this was an era when gunning was an occupation as well as an avocation.

The Mason Decoy Factory, Detroit, Michigan, was the most prolific manufacturer by far. Detroit also spawned the two predecessors of Mason, Peterson and Dodge. H. A. Stevens was the favorite son of Weedsport, New York. For half a century, these four factories supplied hunters with the necessities of life - decoys, weights, and duck calls. How fortunate for us that these men had such a love for wood - for creating decoys, not just making them. There is a world of difference!

For many years, factory decoys, like Rodney Dangerfield, "didn't get no respect!" They were looked upon as the stepchild of the decoy world. Luckily, in recent years the appreciation for their style and beauty has made them highly collectible.

We hope you have as exciting an experience with collecting decoys as we have had. One of the best parts is the fantastic friends you make. Without them, this book would not have been possible. Thanks - to the experienced collectors who helped us when we were starting out, sharing their knowledge and their collections. Thanks - to the friends who allowed their best birds to be included and gave freely of their time. And a special thanks - to Alan Haid, who helped us to proofread and edit; to Bernard Crandell, who shared his extensive knowledge of Mason, Peterson, and Dodge; to George Thompson, who aided us in our Stevens chapter; to Rick Brownlee, whose great drawings will help you identify Masons; and to Frank Klay, who stood out in the cold for hours getting many of the shots you'll find in the book.

Mason Decoys at "Rest." North River, Marshfield, Massachusetts.

MASON
DECOYS

Mason Decoy Factory History & Catalog

Wouldn't William and Herbert Mason be utterly astounded if they could have come back to earth for Richard Bourne's Decoy Auction in July, 1979. Imagine them sitting front row center. I'd love to have seen their faces when the $5,800 opening bid on a pair of Challenge Grade Mergansers was announced! The shock would have sent them scurrying right back to safety. How times have changed!!!

The term factory, according to the Random House Dictionary, means "a building or set of buildings with facilities to manufacture." In this era of vast mechinization and advanced technology, we associate the word factory with large manufacturing plants turning out products on an impersonal assembly line. The Mason Decoy Factory was a factory only in the strictest sense of the word. Compare any ten Premier Mallards and you will notice that no two are exactly alike. Each bears the individual stamp of the men who created it.

The history of the Mason factory has lots of twists and turns, even some blank spots. Thanks to Bernard W. Crandell's excellent and thorough research, much confusion has been dispelled. Mr. Crandell, a resident of the Detroit area and knowledgable decoy man, spent many days searching through old records, visiting sites, and talking to Mason's relatives and employees. His information is invaluable.

William J. Mason, with a partner, George Avery, founded the W. J. Mason Company in 1882. They ran a well equipped sporting goods store which carried a full line of products. They set up shop in the old John E. Long Sporting Goods Store at 133 Jefferson Avenue, Detroit, Michigan. Mason and Avery moved the store to a nearby location in 1888. For reasons unknown, they dissolved the partnership and closed the sporting goods store.

What William Mason did from 1888 to 1896 is not known. Some later Mason advertising states the business was established in 1889, but this has not been verified.

The Mason Decoy Factory had a rather inauspicious start in a shed behind William Mason's house on Tuscola Street. Hardly an indication of his future success. The official date the business was established is 1896, but many feel it was much earlier than this.

William Mason was an excellent hunter and a member of the "Old Club" on Harsen's Island in the St. Clair Flats delta area. This was a sporting club for men who loved to hunt and fish. Who knows? Maybe years of duck hunting convinced him that he could make a better decoy than those available. Those years of studying and observing wild ducks in their natural habitat enabled him to make a decoy which closely resembled its real counterpart.

His decoys proved to be so successful that he moved his decoy business from his home to 456-464 Brooklyn Avenue in 1903. His shop was in the back of the Nicholson Lumber Company. In an interview published in the North American Decoys magazine, Spring-1975, Mr. Crandell talked with Mr. William Kurkowske, a Mason employee from

1904—1906. Much was learned about the workings of the shop at this time.

The building was small and had two floors. The lathes, band saw and sander were downstairs, while upstairs the painting and packing was done. William and Herbert Mason shared an office upstairs. Herbert was responsible for running the factory and doing the paperwork during this time. William was usually out of the office and later died on November 29, 1905, so Herbert took over the family business.

Wagons brought in the cedar logs which were then cut into workable lengths. Patterns were used when cutting the bodies on the lathes. Heads were rough-turned and sanded later. Before taking the decoys upstairs in crates, the head and body were joined.

Upstairs there were three benches with an apprentice and a senior painter at each bench. Drying racks were on each side of the painters. In addition, this is where the puttyers did their work. They filled in around the necks of the Standard Grades decoys with white putty. The fit of the head and body on these grades wasn't perfect, so the putty gave the neck a smooth look. The apprentices put on the primer coat of white lead, linseed oil, and turpentine after the puttying was done and put them on the racks to dry. The senior painter first painted the body with the correct plumage, let it dry, and then painted the head. The glass eyes were added last. Before insertion, the eyes were painted on the back.

On hollow-bodied Premier and Challenge models, white lead sealed the two body parts before being nailed together. When the decoys were completely finished, they were balanced by floating them in a wash tub and adding the lead weight.

All decoys were wrapped separately in newspaper and packed by the dozen in wooden crates. The Premiers had the newspaper they were wrapped in coated with linseed oil. This kept the paper from sticking to the paint. A horse and wagon picked the crates up at the factory.

Mr. Kurkowske, as an apprentice painter, worked ten hours a day, six days a week, for one dollar a day. There was no vacation time or sick pay either. He certainly earned his money.

Business flourished under Herbert Mason's leadership, with unparalled production of duck, goose, and shorebird decoys. William Mason's other sons, Fred and Hugh, were not intimately involved in running the decoy business. Herbert, an avid sportsman like his father, hunted ducks on the St. Clair Flats and the Detroit River. He inherited his father's love and appreciation of waterfowl.

Due to the increased demand for decoys, the Mason Factory moved once again in 1915. Its final location was 5835 Milford Street. The factory only measured 70 feet by 150 feet, with two separate sections. One area for woodworking and the other for the painting. The painting section was closed off to keep the dust from the woodworking area out.

Successful as the business was, it was dependent on seasonal demand. Herbert needed to utilize the factory full-time. He and a friend, Fred Rinshed, a paint salesman, went into business together. They combined the decoys business with paint manufacturing. They incorporated the Rinshed-Mason Company in 1919. Although neither one had experience in paint manufacturing, they hired a chemist and started production. The paint manufacturing became so successful that the decoy operation was closed down in 1924. The twenty-seven year history had come to a close.

Great pride was taken in the making of these birds, "the best decoys made," according to the Mason catalog. You'll find no Mason collector today who will refute that claim.

OR many years the **Mason** models of Decoy Ducks have been recognized by duck shooting authorities as by far the best decoys made.

This applies not only to workmanship, but to the exceptional results obtained by duck shooters who have used these remarkable decoys.

Mason Decoys are made from carefully selected cedar—they are perfect imitations of the live species as to form—and the plumage is imitated so closely as to make it difficult to distinguish them from the live birds, a few feet off.

The **"Premier"** is used by foremost duck shooters everywhere, and the "Standard model Glass Eye" model, slightly lower in price, is a close second in popularity.

Remember high-grade decoys cannot be made in a hurry.

In order to insure prompt shipments we would suggest that order be placed as far in advance of our rush season (September, October and November) as possible.

All leading jobbers and retailers of sporting goods handle our line of **Decoy Ducks** and we refer you to your nearest dealer for quotations.

If you are unable to secure such species or grade as you desire we will be pleased to have you write us direct.

"Premier" Model

Reg. U. S. Patent Office

Hollow and Flat Bottomed. The Finest Ever Made. The drawings for these Decoys were made from life, and as a consequence are mathematically correct, particular attention being paid to all fine details, such as shape of the head, bill, arch of neck, etc. In hollowing them out they are cut in two **above the water line,** thus preventing any leakage. Being flat on the bottom, they ride the water exactly like the living bird, and have not the rocking motion of the old-fashioned decoy in rough weather. The eyes used are the finest enameled glass, colored in exact imitation of those of the living birds. Nothing has been spared to make these goods surpass anything in the shape of a Decoy that has heretofore been manufactured.

MASON DECOYS

CANVAS BACK
PREMIER MODEL
Reg. U. S. Patent Office

Approximate Measurement
of Body
Length - 12½ inches
Width - 6½ inches
Depth - 4½ inches
This pattern is solid model
only.

CANVAS BACK
MAMMOTH CHESAPEAKE BAY
Reg. U. S. Patent Office

RED HEAD
PREMIER MODEL
Reg. U. S. Patent Office

BLUE BILL
PREMIER MODEL
Reg. U. S. Patent Office

MASON DECOYS

MALLARD
PREMIER MODEL
Reg. U. S. Patent Office

BLACK DUCK OR BLACK MALLARD
PREMIER MODEL
Reg. U. S. Patent Office

MASON DECOYS

BLUE WING TEAL   GREEN WING TEAL

PREMIER MODEL
Reg. U. S. Patent Office

SHELL DRAKE

PREMIER MODEL
Reg. U. S. Patent Office

SLEEPING RED HEAD   SLEEPING BLUE BILL

PREMIER MODEL
Reg. U. S. Patent Office

WHISTLER   BUTTER BALL

PREMIER MODEL
Reg. U. S. Patent Office

WIDGEON
PREMIER MODEL
Reg. U. S. Patent Office

SPRIG OR PIN TAIL
PREMIER MODEL
Reg. U. S. Patent Office

STANDARD QUALITY
GLASS EYE
DECOY DUCKS

BLUE BILL

Solid Model only—a first class grade of Cedar Decoy with Glass Eyes—Meets the requirements of those who wish a Decoy, lower in price than our Premier Model and still desire a strictly fine Decoy.

The above grade supplied in Mallard, Black Duck, Blue Bill, Red Head, Canvas Back, Pin or Sprig Tail—Whistler, Widgeon, Blue and Green Wing Teal, Broad Bill.

We can supply other specie on special order.

All of our goods are packed one dozen in a box—8 male, 4 female, to the dozen, **and** we cannot break packages.

BRANT GOOSE

Approximate Measurement
Length   18   inches
Width   7⅜   inches
Depth of Body   5⅛   inches
Depth from top
  of Head   -   9   inches

CROW DECOYS

Here it is!!

The finest Crow Decoy on the market.
It is becoming popular to shoot Crows over
Decoys, especially in closed season on other
birds.

Let us have your order for a few dozen of
these goods, at an early date.

MUD HEN
CHALLENGE MODEL
Reg. U. S. Patent Office

MASON DECOYS

LEAD ANCHORS

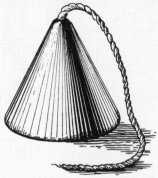 

11W—"WEEDLESS"
Weight, 8 oz. each

11-BS—LONG BRASS SHANK
Weight, 8 oz. each

LEAD BALANCE WEIGHTS

Made of Lead, two holes for fastening the weight to the decoy. Extra hole for attaching anchor cords, thus eliminating the necessity of using rawhide loop or screweyes—this is a combined anchor tie and balance weight—something entirely new and thoroughly practical.

These balance the decoy so it will set upright properly in the water, and are no trouble to attach. Weight about 5 oz. each.

We recommend this weight very highly. We can also supply the old type lead oval body weight.

No. 1A—Japanned
No. 1B—Galvanized
Made from Malleable Iron, with large loop wide enough to go over the head of decoy and small loop for anchor cord.

PRICE LIST

All Quotations F. O. B. Detroit

Subject to change without notice

Model (Hollow) -	$21.00 per dozen
Mammoth Canvas Back (Solid)	21.00 " "
Canada Brant - - - -	30.00 " "
11 W-Weedless Anchors -	2.00 " "
11 BS-Brass Shank Anchors -	2.00 " "
11 BW-Oval Body Weights -	1.50 " "
11 BWX-Oval Body Weights (Extra Heavy) - - -	1.75 " "
11 RHL-Rawhide Loops -	.30 " "
11 SE-Screw Eyes - - -	.15 " "
11 AC-Anchor Cord - -	.50 " "
1 FS-Lead Balance Weight -	1.50 " "
1 J-Iron Loop Anchor - -	2.00 " "
1 G-Iron Loop Anchor -	2.25 " "

These prices for immediate acceptance only

MASON'S DECOY FACTORY
5971-5 Milford St. & P. M. R. R.
DETROIT, MICHIGAN

Masons For The Beginning Collector

Welcome to the wild, exciting world of Mason collectors. A more interested or interesting group of people is hard to find. Avid collectors - rather an understatement!!! Get ready for decoy lists flying through the mail, for decoy shows all over the country, for crazy calls at crazy times, and most of all, for the most fantastic decoys in the world.

Although a "factory" decoy, their beauty is unsurpassed. Superb painting and classic body lines earn them their mark of distinction. The artistic touch is clearly evident when you study the fine painting technique. This must of been more than just a job to these men in the paint shop. The extra care taken with the stippling and swirling, with the subtle color variations, and with the hand carved heads surely proves this was also a means of self expression. They were truly artists.

Because of the many grades of Mason decoys, each with its own characteristics, a beginning collector needs to learn which qualities identify each grade. The best collector is an informed collector.

Grades of Masons

The Mason Decoy Factory made several grades of decoys. It continues to confuse us today. The Mason catalog lists five grades: Premier, Challenge, No. 1 Glass Eye, No. 2 Tack Eye, and No. 3 Painted Eye. The confusion centers on the last three grades, which are commonly called Standard Grades.

Collectors use the terms "Detroit" Grade and "3rd" Grade for the No. 1 Glass Eye and "4th" Grade for the No. 3 Painted Eye. No one is positive how the terms evolved, but they are widely used. Each of the grades will be discussed in detail to help you in the identification of your decoys. Happy hunting!

Premier Grade

The Premier Grade is the top of the line, as the name suggests. It has all the extras one would expect to find in the finest decoy. The Premier is characterized by a full, graceful body, a beautifully carved head and bill, and a spectacular paint job.

The paint was lavishly applied, rich in color yet very durable. Swirls in the paint were created by deft strokes of the brush, adding that special quality to these factory decoys. Many Premier species, such as the Mallard Drake, have the swirl painting on the breast, a definite plus in any decoy. Delicate color variations helped to make these birds accurate duplications of nature. True artisans, the painters expertly applied the speckling, stippling, and the feathering. Stippling, small white flecks of paint on the body, was added at the factory. This is not to be confused with overpaint. Feathering is found on the back of the body on some species; they are thin lines the shape of the crescent moon.

The richly textured, high quality paint has withstood the ravages of man and water. Decoys in good original paint are enjoyed seventy-five years later. It has been said that Mason used "special" paint for his decoys, but this is not so. They used the conventional paint manufactured in their own factory. The same paint they supplied Ford Motor

25

Company. Mellowed by time and weather, Mason Premiers glow with a patina modern carvers cannot duplicate.

Mason advertising featured hollow, flat-bottomed construction in all Premiers, unless specifically ordered to be solid. The upswept tail and round body enhanced its flowing lines. The bodies were hollowed out above the water line to prevent water from leaking into the decoy. You will see a thin line running horizontally around the decoy. The flat bottom allowed it to ride the water like a wild duck, although not all hunters attest to that theory. The hollow construction took more time and skill, thus they were more expensive. If you've ever carried dozens of wooden decoys across a mile of plowed ground in bitter cold, you know why hollow ones were so desirable.

Solid body Premiers were special orders and would have been used in rougher water. The solid body enabled it to ride more smoothly in the water. They incorporated all the desirable features of the top grade, yet were practical for the conditions rougher water creates.

Premier Grade decoys are distinguished by notched bill carving and a separate "nail" carving on the end of the bill. Good enameled glass eyes were used to duplicate the color of the live duck's eyes.

Obviously, when you combine hollow construction, superb paint, and elaborate bill carving you have all the qualities expected in a superior decoy. Premier Grade is truly an accurate description of these wonderful birds.

Top view of four grades of Masons

Challenge Grade

While not a twin, the Challenge Grade Mason is definitely a first cousin to the Premier Grade. Although Challenge was Mason's second best grade of decoy, some collectors prefer its sleeker, more streamlined look. The full body with the upswept tail, the carved bill, and the exceptional paint make these decoys winners.

Although the body style is very similar to the Premier, the Challenge Grade's is not quite as full and plump. Each body dimension is slightly smaller. The majority of Challenge Masons are solid, although a hollow model could be specially ordered. The hollow models have the thin line running horizontally around the body like the Premier. A hollow-bodied Challenge Grade is more desirable to some because of its rarity. Be on the lookout!

The key to identifying the Challenge Mason is the carved line which separates the head and the bill. A groove which separates the mandibles is also found. Carved nostrils are on the top of the bill.

Many Challenge Grades are found with "snaky" heads. Its long slender bill and racy style differs from the traditional head. The underside of the head, from the bill to the neck, is thinner and more delicate. The top of the bill has more of an upward curve. Now all you have to do is find a "snaky" head on a hollow Challenge. You'll really have it made!

If you've ever seen a hollow Challenge Merganser, with its snaky head and wonderfully carved comb, you're lucky. Painted with absolute abandon, you can understand why this might be an owner's favorite. That snaky head gives the feeling of motion. You can almost feel the wind as it glides through the water.

The quality of paint of the Challenges compares favorably with the Premiers. The realistic coloration, feathering, swirling, and stippling are found on this grade also. Paint swirls on the breast are found on many of the species. Mason marked the bottom of the Premier and Challenge Grades with a stamp that said Challenge - Reg. U.S. Pat. Office or Premier - Reg. U.S. Pat. Office. During use this stamp was worn off and it is hard to find one with the original stencil. The ones we've found have been on decoys used sparingly or those overpainted on the bottom.

We found a snaky head Challenge Black Duck that was overpainted on the bottom with a brownish wash. (This practice was fairly common in New England. The overpaint protected against the effects of salt water.) The rest of the decoy was in its original condition. When the wash was removed, you can imagine our surprise to find the Challenge stencil. Evidently, when the hunter received his shipment of decoys, he put a thin coat of paint on the bottom, unwittingly preserving the stamp.

Premier stamp

Challenge stamp

If the number of Challenge Grade decoys is compared to the number of Premier Grades found, we can assume the Premier was the more popular of the two. For a few dollars more per dozen, the more affluent hunters must have gone all the way and bought the "top of the line." Because of its relative scarcity and quality workmanship, collectors frequently cherish their Challenge Grades more and sometimes pay more for them.

Standard Grade Masons

"Detroit" Grade, "4th" Grade, Painted Eye, Tack Eye, "3rd" Grade, Glass Eye-----Help!!!!! Learning the various names for the three Standard Grades is like trying to master the colloquialisms in French I. You think you have it straight when you hear another term - for the same thing. Hopefully, this section will help you before you become mired in despair.

The Standard Grades are listed in the Mason Catalogs and price lists as No. 1 Glass Eye, No. 2 Tack Eye, and No. 3 Painted Eye, in descending order of quality and price. Because the Standard Grades were less than half the cost of the Premier and Challenge Grades, the average, "working man" hunter could more easily afford to own a dozen or more of them. He received a good decoy for a reasonable price.

A more detailed description of each grade's characteristics follows. The drawings and pictures point out important features to look for when identifying the Standard Grades.

No. 1 Glass Eye

The Glass Eye is the classiest of the Standard Grade trio, which accounts for its popularity with hunters and collectors alike. Commonly called "Detroit" Grade or "3rd" Grade, this is the Mason most likely to be found on collector's shelves. Their price and style put them in great demand with hunters across the country in the early 1900's, thus assuring today's collector an ample supply from which to choose.

This grade gets its name from the fine, enameled glass eyes Mason used. It is their 3rd best grade of decoy and the only Standard Grade that always has glass eyes.

The body of the "Detroit" Grade is smaller than the Premier and Challenge in every dimension. You find a tail that is squared off and straight, rather than upswept. The bill lacks any carving. The bill is defined only through the use of paint. Some species, such as the Blue Bill, have the nostrils and the tip of the bill painted black. The head and body styles vary according to the species. It is important to study the sections on the individual species so you will be familiar with its form and paint style. The Mason decoys were made to closely resemble its counterpart in nature.

The painting of the "Detroit" Grade is far superior to the two lower grades. Swirls in the paint are not usually found. In those species that have breast paint, such as the Canvas Back Drake, the breast paint is scalloped like the Premier and Challenge.

The price difference between the Glass Eye and the Tack Eye was less than one dollar a dozen so hunters must have felt the superior quality was worth the extra expense. You be the judge.

No. 2 Tack Eye

One step down in overall quality is the Tack Eye. The name for this grade comes from the metal tacks used for eyes. The tacks were inserted after the decoy was painted because you can see the putty around the eye is unpainted. There are two identifying features to look for: the tack eyes and the paint style.

The durability of the paint was comparable to the "Detroit" Grade, but the finer, artistic details are missing. A straight line defines the breast, in some species, rather than breast swirls or scallops.

Some species are identical to the Glass Eye, except for the tack eyes. Other species also lack the feathering and the stippling found on the Glass Eye counterparts.

As mentioned before, the Glass Eye could be purchased for less than a dollar more, so the demand for the Tack Eyes was not so great. The hunters must have felt the Glass Eyes decoyed better or felt the paint was more realistic. Whatever the reason, a Tack Eye Mason in excellent condition is hard to find!

No. 3 Painted Eye

The Painted Eye or "4th" Grade was the lowest grade of Mason decoy available. Rumor has it that the Painted Eye was made from rejects or seconds of the other grades. A mistake may have been made in carving or the quality of the cedar might not have been good enough for the higher grades. Thus, the "mistakes" became Painted Eye decoys.

The Painted Eye has a long, tube-like body. The body is not as wide or as deep as the other two Standard Grades. This, along with the painted eyes, makes this grade distinctive.

As you must suspect by its name, the "4th" Grades have painted eyes. The eyes are either orange or yellowish-orange with a black dot in the middle. Occasionally, this grade is found with glass eyes. The eyes may have been added at the factory in order to improve its appearance, thus making it more saleable.

Although the Painted Eye lacks the fine details and style found in the other Mason decoys, its naive charm alone makes it an important member of any collection.

Because less time was spent on the carving of the Standard Grades, the fit of the head to the body was not perfect. Putty was filled in where the head joined the neck before the primer coat of paint was applied. The putty was later covered by the coats of paint. A Standard Grade Mason with the neck filler intact is much more desirable and more valuable.

Early Style Vs. Later Style

During the years the Mason Decoy Factory was in operation, the body and head style changed greatly. The early birds had an exaggerated, sloped breast and a flat bottom. The head was much cheekier than the later models.

As time passed, the breast became less pronounced and the head and body sleeker. The underside of the head, between the bill and the neck, became more concave. The photographs clearly illustrate the difference between the two styles. The earlier Masons are not necessarily more collectible or valuable because most collectors prefer the later Masons. Beauty is in the eye of the collector!

Front view of Premier and Challenge Grade Masons

Front view of Standard Grade Mason

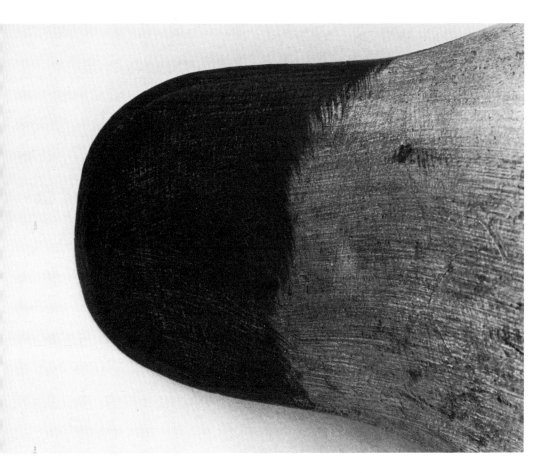

Characteristic brush strokes on underside of Mason decoy.

Characteristic swirls in Mason paint. Note the feathering on the back.

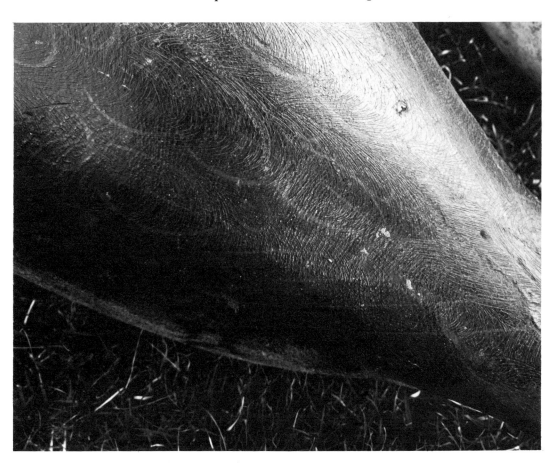

This shows the size variances of Mason decoys. The size is in proportion to the live duck.

Black Duck

This is the species where it's a snap to tell the hen and drake apart. Since the wild hen Black Duck or Black Mallard has the same coloration as her male counterpart, Mason only produced one decoy for each grade. Using the same head and body as the Mallard, Mason clearly shows on the Black Duck the mastery they had achieved with brush and paint.

The Standard Grade Black Duck, unlike some other species, has much the appeal of the Premier and Challenge Grade models. The feathering found all over the body adds highlights to the black body, while the green speculum adds a dash of bright color. The light brown speckled head, accented by black eye markings, is a direct color contrast to the dark body.

Study the brush strokes and the application of the fine details and you will understand why Mason decoys are renowned for their superior painting technique and artistry.

You might assume the collecting of Black Ducks would be unchallenging, but the variety of head and body styles in each grade proves this assumption wrong. At last count, a friend in Connecticut had sixteen Black Ducks, each one different from the next. We lined them up on the floor one time and what a sight that made! From early style to late style, from Painted Eye to Premier Grade, and even a twenty-four inch oversize Black. Go ye out and search. Maybe you can find seventeen - or more.

A Mason trio—Glass Eye Black Duck, Tack Eye Black Duck and Challenge Black Duck.

Mason Challenge Black Duck, early slope breasted style

Mason Premier Grade Black Duck

Mason Glass Eye Black Duck

Mason Painted Eye Black Duck

Mason Premier Grade Black Duck   Mason hollow Challenge Grade Black Duck.

Mason Tack Eye Black Duck

Mason Challenge Grade Black Duck, snaky head and challenge stamp

Blue Bills

Subtlety would be a key word in describing Mason Blue Bills or Scaup. Not dazzling like a Merganser or Pintail, not wildly colorful like a Widgeon or Mallard, the Blue Bill excells in style. What appears to be a black-and-white bird at a distance, shows upon close examination, black, white, gray, and a beautiful brown of the sides of the Premier and Challenge Grade Drakes. The hen's soft browns and whites blend together beautifully. This blending of colors, combined with variations in style, make this a favorite of many.

Greater Scaup or Broad Bills and Lesser Scaup or Blue Bills were popular items on the Mason Decoy Factory "bill of fare." Some confusion exists because collectors group them together as Blue Bills, while Mason lists them separately as Broad Bill and Blue Bill in the catalog. They are alike except for the width of their bill. The Broad Bill has a wide bill with a flare at the end the shape of a light bulb. The Blue Bill has a narrower bill with little flaring at the end.

Several variations in style make this species a good one to collect. The five grades in both Broad Bill and Blue Bill are offered, as well as "low-head" sleepers and oversize and undersize models. The "low-head" models are confined to two species, Blue Bills and Red Heads; both Premier and Challenge Grades were featured in this contented head position. While the Standard Grades lack the finer paint detailing of the higher grades, a jaunty air makes them quite appealing. The Blue Bills are understated beauties!

Rare Hollow Mason Challenge Grade Blue Bill Hen

Pair of Mason Challenge Grade Blue Bills

Pair of early style Mason Blue Bills - Challenge Grade

Pair of Mason Glass Eye Blue Bills

Mason Premier Broad Bill Hen

Pair of Mason Premier Grade Blue Bills

Mason Challenge Grade Blue Bill Drake

Mason Tack Eye Blue Bill Hen

Mason Tack Eye Blue Bill Drake

Pair of "special order" solid body Premier Blue Bills

Pair of Mason Painted Eye Blue Bills

Brant, Goose, and Swan

A more impressive trio of Masons would be hard to find! Quite large decoys, they give a majestic touch to any collection. Both the Brant and Goose were offered in Premier and Challenge Grades only and all had solid bodies.

The Brant or Brant Goose was found along the East and West Coast and has a smaller body and shorter bill than the Canada Goose. Because there was only regional interest in Brant, the production was somewhat limited even though it was a featured item in the catalog. The Mason Brant, on the other hand, enjoys universal interest from Maine to California.

Big, bold, and beautiful - the Mason Canada Goose is prized by collectors as much as the live goose is prized by the hunter. One of the most cautious birds, the goose was hard to bring down and a good decoy was essential. Compared to the number of geese hunted, the number of decoys found is small for a couple of reasons. Many areas used live decoys or tollers instead of wooden blocks and the weight of these large birds was limited by the number the hunter could carry.

In order to entice the geese, the decoys had to closely resemble the live bird in form and coloring. Using that criterion, a Mason Goose is so fine it could attract a gaggle of geese. Who knows? Maybe the apprentice painters practiced the swirling of paint on the goose because it is wonderfully prominent. Bold feathering accentuates the plump body. What self-respecting goose wouldn't have been attracted by this charmer?

The Swan, one of the rarest Mason decoys, was used in the Mid-Atlantic area. Swans were hunted for their down and their feathers until 1913 when their slaughter was outlawed. The swan then found use as a "confidence" decoy. Placed with the rig of ducks, a swan decoy gave a false assurance of safety to other birds. While the years have taken their toll on the paint, nothing can diminish the majesty of the Mason Swan.

Mason Challenge Grade Brant

44

Mason Premier Goose

Mason Goose

Mason Goose

Mason Goose

Mason Brant

Mason Challenge Grade Brant

Bufflehead (Butter Ball)

It's a shame the Bufflehead wasn't hunted more heavily because the Mason Bufflehead decoys are exceptionally impressive. They were not the choice of the market hunters or sportsmen because of their small size, so few decoys were needed in the rig. Also, the Bufflehead, not very choosy about the company it kept, would decoy to other species. Infrequently found, especially the hen, Mason Buffleheads are a real find. While never found in a Premier or Painted Eye model, you never know what might turn up some day.

Mason used Teal heads and bodies on these little birds, just varying the paint pattern. The hen, painted in shades of brown and white, pales in contrast to the drake, a study in black and white. His white head patch resembles a crown, with white wing patches adding a final regal touch.

Mason Swan

Pair of Mason Challenge Grade Buffleheads, hen and drake.

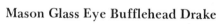

Mason Glass Eye Bufflehead Drake

Pair of Mason Challenge Grade Buffleheads

Mason Challenge Grade Bufflehead Hen

Canvas Backs

Collectors across the country are out to "bag" these spectacular decoys for their shelves. This regal bird, with its low, sloping forehead and long bill, was a favorite of the market hunter. Canvasbacks, a good table bird, brought top dollar at the wholesale market, so the men who made their living gunning were out to kill them in volume. Both market gunners and sportsmen needed a good block to decoy the birds, and each area of the country had special requirements due to the type of water over which they hunted. This presented Mason with a challenge - making a variety of styles to meet these specifications. His success kept the production team busy!

Mason met these regional requirements by making a Seneca Lake model, a Mammoth Chesapeake Bay model, solid body Premiers, and large body Premiers. These were in addition to the full line of regular grades of Canvas Backs. The Seneca Lake model, with its high neck and large body, was used in the choppy waters of the Seneca Lake area of New York. The Mammoth Chesapeake Bay model had an erect head and an oversized, solid body: it was used in the rough waters of the eastern shore of Maryland.

One of our long-time favorites, the Mason Canvas Back commands the respect of all. The contrast of the deep red and black against the white accentuates the beautiful form of the drake, while the hen, with her subtle browns and whites, exemplifies nature's camouflage. They make a winsome pair, indeed!

Unused pair of Mason Painted Eye Canvas Backs - Drake and Hen

Mason Premier Canvas Backs with small bodies and snaky heads.

Mason Challenge Canvas Backs.

Special order Mason oversize Canvas Back Drake

Pair of Mason Chesapeake Bay Canvas Backs

Pair of Mason Premier Grade Canvas Backs - Seneca Lake style

55

Mason Premier Grade Seneca Lake Canvas Back Hen and Drake

Mason Tack Eye Canvas Back Drake

Mason Premier Grade Canvas Back Hen

Pair of Mason Premier Grade Canvas Backs

Mason Challenge Grade Canvas Back Hen with hollow body

Pair of Mason Painted Eye Canvas Backs

Pair of Mason Glass Eye Canvas Backs

Coot and Scoter

Coots would never win the Phi Beta Kappa key for the bird world. In fact they are just plain dumb! Not true ducks, Coots belong to the rail family of small wading birds. Slow-moving and slow-witted, they like to join the ducks, so Coot decoys added a touch of realism to the rig. Although they were hunted, they tasted awful. They didn't get the name Mud Hen for nothing. More likely, they were used for target practice.

Mason Coots were featured in the catalog and came in Challenge Grade only. Their white bill, their black and gray body, and their alert head make them very distinctive. Unfortunately, the upturned tail was susceptible to damage and it's hard to find one without a tail chip. A very appealing decoy, so hope you can add one to your collection.

A sea duck used to rough water, the Scoter was hunted on the East Coast. Mason offered the White Wing Scoter and the Surf Scoter but few have been found. New England hunters were very independent and often made their own decoys. Some were too poor for the "store bought" variety. Those that were ordered had a hard time surviving the elements. Sea water was hard on paint so an original paint Scoter is very special!

Mason Coots. Rare gray Coot, regular style Coot, and high neck Coot. All Challenge Grade Masons.

Mason Coot

Mason Coot

Mason White Wing Scoter

Mason Gray Coot

Goldeneye (Whistler)

The Goldeneye, named for its bright yellow eyes, was hunted primarily in the Northeast, although it's seen as far west as Michigan. This diver made for good shooting and decoyed well, hence all five grades have been found. A whistling sound made by the wings when in flight earned it the nickname Whistler. Whatever name you choose, it is a striking decoy.

Like many Masons, form and shape alone can be used to identify Goldeneyes. A slight pointedness to the head and a thicker bill are good features to note. The hen Goldeneye closely resembles the hen Canvas Back in coloring but the head shape and the color of the eyes is different. As in most other species, the drake basks in the limelight, coming to you in glorious black and white. White, circular cheek patches lend a whimsical touch. Who wouldn't love a pair?

Two Mason Challenge Grade Goldeneye Drakes

Pair of Mason Challenge Grade Goldeneyes.

Pair of Mason Challenge Grade Goldeneyes

Mason Glass Eye Goldeneye Drake

Mason Premier Grade Goldeneye Hen

Mason Premier Grade Goldeneye Drake

Mason Glass Eye Goldeneye Hen

Mason Painted Eye Goldeneye Hen

Mallard

The Mallard decoy was the staple of most carver's inventory and Mason was no exception. Certainly the Mason most commonly found, this species represents one of their best efforts. Mallards offer great variety: early slope-breasted Premiers, snaky head Challenge Grades. This affords the collector a unique opportunity. One could collect Mason Mallards exclusively for years without duplicating another decoy exactly.

For many years, Mallards were featured in Mason's national advertising literature. Because the wild Mallard was commonly found throughout North America, it must have been one of their best sellers, as they've been found from coast to coast.

A rainbow of colors makes this a favorite of many collectors; it is often the choice for those who want one or two "mantle" birds. The wonderful variety of paint patterns a and head and body styles, especially on the Premiers, make these decoys a collector's dream.

Pair of Mason Challenge Grade Mallards with snaky heads and hollow bodies

A Pair of Early Style Mason Mallard Hens—One Premier and One Challenge Grade.

Pair of Mason Glass Eye Mallards

Pair of Mason Painted Eye Mallards

Early style Mason Challenge Grade Mallard Hen

Unusual head style, Mason Premier Grade Mallard Drake

Mason Premier Grade Mallard Hen

Pair of Premier Grade Mallards

Pair of Mason Challenge Grade Mallards

Mason Premier Grade Mallards - Drake and Hen

Merganser (Sheldrake)

"Floating sculpture," an interesting term that's used to describe decoys in general, is a made-to-order description of Mason Premier and Challenge Sheldrakes. Superb in style, wonderful in color, these decoys have a decidedly elegant look. With their slender "saw bill," their distinguished crest, and their long, lean body, they almost appear to be in suspended animation, waiting for that moment of freedom on the water. Even the Standard Grade Sheldrakes have a special quality to them.

Patterned after the Red-breasted Merganser, a fish-eater, these decoys are rarely found today. The wild duck, because of its fishy taste, was not widely hunted, so it's not surprising so few Mason Sheldrakes are found. Perhaps this very scarcity makes owning one so very special! So far, we haven't had the priviledge, but hope springs eternal.

Mason Challenge Grade Merganser Drake and Hen.

Mason Premier Grade Merganser Drake

Mason Tack Eye Merganser Drake

Pair of Mason Glass Eye Mergansers

Mason Challenge Grade Merganser Drake with hollow body

Mason Challenge Grade Merganser Drake

Mason Challenge Grade Merganser Hen

79

Old Squaw

A "special order" decoy, the Mason Old Squaw was designed to meet the regional needs of the East Coast. While it's considered a Sea Duck, it is also found on many large inland lakes and rivers.

Not especially tasty, they were generally ignored by the market hunters. It was hard to ignore their incessant chattering, which supposedly is the reason they were named Old Squaw.

The Mason Decoy Factory filled these special orders by using a little ingenuity. They used the Premier Pintail body and head, modifying the head by shortening the bill. The black and white paint pattern of the drake was used. No hen Old Squaws have ever been found, though that's not to say they were never made. Its long, slender tail and striking paint make this rarely found decoy an exceptionally pleasing decoy.

Typical scalloped breast paint found on many species of Masons.

Mason Challenge Grade Old Squaw Drake

Mason Premier Grade Old Squaw Drake

Pintail

With its long, pointed tail and slender head and body, the Mason Pintail or Sprig seems too exotic to be classified as a mere working decoy. Can't imagine a hunter casually throwing them in a basket with the rest of the rig. Hey! Watch the paint!

Even in silhouette, the unique form of the Pintail makes it easily identifible. The drake's longer tail and white head marking lend a stately air. With her shorter, stubbier tail and muted coloring, the hen makes a deserving consort.

The migratory routes of the Pintail took them over California and the Mississippi Flyway where hunters sought to decoy these fleet birds within their range. These sleek, slender-necked decoys must have proved as irresistible to the wild duck as they have been to the collector. Factory decoy or not, the Mason Pintail is a decoy classic.

Mason Challenge Grade Pintail Drake

Mason Challenge Grade Pintail Hen

Mason Tack Eye Pintail Hen and Drake

Mason Premier Grade Pintail Hen.

Pair of Mason Painted Eye Pintails

Pair of Mason Premier Grade Pintails

Mason Challenge Grade Pintail Hen - hollow body

Mason Glass Eye Pintail Drake

Early style Mason Premier Pintail Hen

87

Red Head

The Red Head, prized for its meat during the market hunting era, was a prime target for the battery or sinkbox shooters. Red Heads, as well as Canvasbacks, brought top dollar at market, thus ensuring their widespread massacre.

A battery was a floating box which sat very low in the water. Iron wing ducks sat on the canvas-covered platforms that surrounded the box and kept the battery at water level. With hundreds of ducks surrounding the sinkbox, the hunter would lay on his back until the ducks were in shooting range. Up he'd sit and Red Heads would fall - sometimes by the hundreds. Masons, no doubt, brought down their fair share. Good for collectors because there are many available, but it spelled near extinction for the Red Head. Even today, hunters are severely limited in the number they may shoot.

Mason Red Heads have as much variety as the local Five and Dime. It's difficult deciding which head and body style you prefer. If luck is with you, a sleeper or "low-head" will grace your shelf. Unlike the wild duck, it's open season on Mason Red Heads.

Mason Glass Eye Red Head Hen. This was found in an attic wrapped in a 1921 newspaper. It was never weighted or used.

Early head style, Mason Challenge Grade Red Head Hen

Early head style, Challenge Grade Red Head Drake

Mason Premier Grade Red Head Hen.

Pair of Mason Premier Grade Red Heads

Pair of Mason Premier Grade Red Heads

Pair of Mason Painted Eye Red Heads

Mason Glass Eye Hen and Drake Red Heads

Mason Challenge Grade Red Head Drake and Hen

Mason Tack Eye Red Head Drake

Mason Tack Eye Red Head Hen

Blue Wing and Green Wing Teal

Some of the most sought after Mason decoys are Blue Wing and Green Wing Teal. These diminutive birds were lavishly painted - no detail was omitted. Teal are swift flying birds that decoy well, and they make delicious eating. They prefered the fresh waters of the Midwest and the Pacific Flyways, so this is where Mason Teal are usually found. The fresh water was easier on the paint, so many Teal are found in excellent condition.

The Mason Blue Wing Teal, found primarily in the Midwest, is much more common than the Green Wing. Available in all five grades, the Premier and Challenge models are finely carved and exquisitely painted. A large, white crescent accents the gray head of the drake. The reddish breast is speckled and the speculum is green, with cobalt blue shoulder feathers. The hen is dark brown on top, with a speckled light brown head and breast. Like the drake, the speculum is green and the shoulder feathers blue. The three Standard Grade Teal have a different paint pattern than the Premier and Challenge Grades. The Glass Eye and Tack Eye are speckled and have only a blue speculum and no shoulder feathers. The Painted Eye Blue Wing lacks the speckling and has a blue speculum. The Mason Blue Wing makes up in beauty what it lacks in size.

Finding a Green Wing Teal is like Jason finding the Golden Fleece - difficult but not impossible! Once a collector owns one, it's like the marriage vow - 'til death do us part. The drake Green Wing has a gorgeous chestnut head and a green patch behind each eye; the speculum is green. The hen looks very similar to the Blue Wing except for the green speculum. The Green Wing Teal do not have the shoulder feathers that the Blue Wings have.

Best of luck in your quest for a Green Wing! And if you ever decide to sell yours - give us a call! We're in the book.

Mason Premier Green Wing Teal Drake.

Pair of Mason Tack Eye Blue Wing Teal.

Pair of Mason Glass Eye Blue Wing Teal

Mason Premier Grade Blue Wing Teal Drake

Mason Premier Grade Blue Wing Teal Drake

Mason Premier Grade Blue Wing Teal Hen.   Pair of Mason Glass Eye Green Wing Teal.

Mason Challenge Grade Blue Wing Teal Drake

Mason Challenge Grade Blue Wing Teal Drake

Mason Challenge Grade Blue Wing Teal Hen

Mason Premier Grade Blue Wing Teal Drake

Mason Premier Grade Green Wing Teal Hen

Mason Painted Eye Blue Wing Teal

Pair of Mason Challenge Grade Blue Wing Teal

Assortment of Blue Wing Teal

Widgeon

A loud mouth and an occasional thief, the Widgeon would not win a popularity contest with hunters or other ducks. But a Mason Widgeon - now that's another story!

Widgeon quickly warned other ducks of danger with a loud whistle, infuriating many a hunter. Not very adept at diving for food, they are known to steal food from the bills of other ducks when they surface. Luckily, Mason collectors don't hold this against them.

The brilliantly colorful drake is a show-stopper. The white crown gives him a bald-headed look, thus the name Baldpate. Green eye patches and a red breast give him a rather dashing appearance, while the hen is dull in comparison. Their bill is rather short and stubby, but they certainly make a fine couple.

Mason Widgeon are rare and are treasured by those lucky enough to own them. We had given up on finding a Tack Eye Widgeon for the book. We were rooting around the storage room at the Shelburne Museum where they keep the extra decoys not on display. Sitting there, grungy and forlorn, was a Tack Eye Drake. We offered to give it a good home but they declined, so we settled for a picture. Better something than nothing.

Mason Premier Grade Widgeon Drake and Challenge Grade Hen and Drake

Mason Glass Eye Widgeon Drake.

Pair of Mason Challenge Grade Widgeons

Mason Premier Grade Widgeons

102

Mason Tack Eye Widgeon Drake

Mason Premier Grade Widgeon Drake

Mason Premier Grade Widgeon Drake

Mason Premier Grade Widgeon Hen

Two Old Coots—The Human Variety.

Wood Duck

The ultimate decoy in beauty and rarity. Not discriminating about his friends, this woodland duck would decoy to other species, so a hunter had little use for a Wood Duck decoy. A few "special orders" have been found and they are richly colored and well executed. Too bad Wood Ducks were such gullible birds. If not, maybe there would be more of these beauties to enjoy!

Mason Challenge Grade Wood Duck Hen

Rare Mason Tack Eye Wood Duck Drake

Mason Tack Eye Wood Duck Drake

Shorebirds

Skittering across the shoreline, bobbing their heads up and down, shore birds seem to have limitless energy. Almost gunned into extinction prior to the 1920's, these naive birds decoyed very easily during the fall and spring shooting seasons. All we have left of the Eskimo Curlew is the decoy. For them, conservation came too late.

Coming in a variety of sizes, colors and shapes, Mason Shore Birds closely duplicate the real bird. Similar coloration on shore birds makes it difficult to distinguish the different species at times. Hopefully, the color pictures and descriptions will help you.

Mason offered two grades of shore birds: A-1 or Glass Eye and B-2 or Tack Eye. The Glass Eye was more expensive but the painting details and technique were superior. Eight species were offered: Golden Plover, Yellowlegs, Black-bellied Plover, Jacksnipe, Dowitcher, Willet, Robin Snipe and Curlew. Many were available in fall and spring plumage and "special order" shore birds have been found.

Collecting Mason Shore Birds is like eating peanuts. It's impossible to stop at just one. They're fast becoming our favorites!

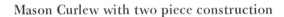

Mason Curlew with two piece construction

Mason Special Order Black-bellied Plover in fall plumage

Mason Black-bellied Plover in spring plumage

107

Plovers

Plovers generally have shorter bills than Snipe and their bodies are shorter and plumper, with a short, thick neck.

BLACK - BELLIED PLOVER: This species in spring plumage is easily identified by its black belly and white forehead, underbody and sides. The "special order" Beetlehead in fall plumage is quite rare. This is a superb example of Mason's quality workmanship.

GOLDEN PLOVER: Look for the short bill and the golden brown coloring. The head and wing are darker brown with yellow specks.

Curlew

Most magnificent Mason Shore Bird by far! Two species were offered - Long Bill or Sickle Bill and Hudsonian or Short Bill. They were made with one and two piece bodies. Their slender, arched necks and elongated bodies are unmistakable.

Snipe

YELLOWLEGS: Probably the most common Mason Shore Bird, you'll find them with numerous paint variations. All have a long iron bill and a long, thin body. It is very similar to the Willet, but the Yellowlegs usually has a smaller body. Although most shore birds are found near the coast, eight Yellowlegs were found in Wisconsin with the original sticks. Some transplanted hunter probably couldn't bear to part with his.

WILLET: With a brown back in spring plumage and a gray back in fall plumage, the Willet is not very colorful, yet it's certainly not a plain Jane. Looking like a Yellowlegs, it has a bigger body generally. A simple, stylish bird.

Mason Glass Eye Golden Plover in foreground, Glass Eye Dowitcher in the back.

DOWITCHER: Not a common shore bird, the Dowitcher has a long bill and a large body. Three rare split tail feeding Dowitchers were found one cold morning at a Massachusetts flea market. "I'm keeping the best pair for myself," said the old gentleman selling them. Who can argue with that logic? Nevertheless, we're still trying to get them!

ROBIN SNIPE: Also known as a Knot, this very pleasing decoy has a burnt umber breast. One of the more uncommon and desirable of Mason Shore Birds.

JACK SNIPE: There are only two examples of the Mason Jack Snipe known. The one pictured resembles the one in the Mason catalog exactly. The two that were found were bought out of an antique shop on Long Island, so keep beating the bushes. Who knows when another will turn up.

Page from Mason Catalog.

MASON'S DECOY FACTORY   DETROIT, MICHIGAN

SHORE BIRDS IN TWO GRADES

A-1.—Enamel glass eyes.   B-2—Tack eyes
12-inch sticks for legs furnished

ROBIN SNIPE   GOLDEN PLOVER   YELLOW LEGS   BLACK BREAST   SNIPE

WILLET

LONG BILL CURLEW   DOWITCHER
CHALLENGE MODEL
Reg. U. S. Patent Office

Rare Mason Shore Birds.

Mason Long Bill Curlew

Mason Tack Eye Golden Plover.

Mason Glass Eye Black-bellied Plover

Mason Curlew

Mason Glass Eye Robin Snipe (Knot)

111

Shore bird hunting in Marshfield, Mass, about 1900.

Mason Tack Eye Willet in spring plumage.

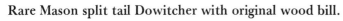

Rare Mason split tail Dowitcher with original wood bill.

Mason Tack Eye Golden Plover.

Mason Special Orders & Rarities

Special Orders and Rarities

<u>SPECIAL ORDERS</u>

Many "special orders" were filled by the Mason Decoy Factory over the years. The Old Squaw and the Wood Duck are two already mentioned. A hunter could order a species not normally offered or order a change of style on a decoy, as an oversize body or a variation in a head style.

<u>Special order</u> - Whistler Hen and Canvas Back Drake

These little decoys were obviously painted by Mason but designed by someone who had their own notion of what a decoy should look like. They are real charmers!

<u>Special order</u> - Oversize Decoys

Canvas Backs and Black Ducks have been found with oversized bodies. These are not to be confused with the Mammoth Chesapeake Bay models. Some of the Black Ducks have twenty-four inch bodies and these decoys were probably used in rougher water.

Rarities

<u>SLEEPERS OR LOW-HEADS</u> - These rare decoys have only been found in two species - Blue Bills and Red Heads. These contented birds were made in Challenge and Premier Grade only. They gave false sense of security to wild ducks flying over the rig. They are wonderful in style and unique in their charm.

<u>CROW</u> - Mason's example of this well-known bird is folky and rarely found in collections. Pure black, the Mason Crow must have fooled many with its craning stance. Even though they were advertised in later catalogs, very few have been discovered.

<u>DOVE</u> - Popular as game birds, especially in the South, doves were hunted heavily until 1913 when they were classed as a migratory bird, thus ensuring their survival.

The Mason Dove looks very similar to several of Mason's other shore birds in shape and coloring so it's difficult to distinguish. A dove is a prized addition to any shore bird collection.

<u>SALESMAN'S SAMPLES</u> - Aren't those Mason Miniature Mallards on the cover fabulous? They're believed to be salesman's samples (c. 1910) and are exact duplicates of the Premier Grade Mallard - hen and drake. If those walked in the door, I'd want to stock Masons in my store, that's for sure!!! The paint is original, executed in exquisite detail. Two other samples have supposedly been found - a Premier Wood Duck and a Premier Canvas Back Drake. Why can't we ever find something like that?

Pair of Mason Glass Eye Yellowlegs

Rare Mason Split-Tail feeding Dowitcher

Mason Oversize Willet

114

Pair of Mason Low-Head Premier Blue Bills

Mason Special Order Whistler Hen   Mason Crow

115

Mason Dove

116

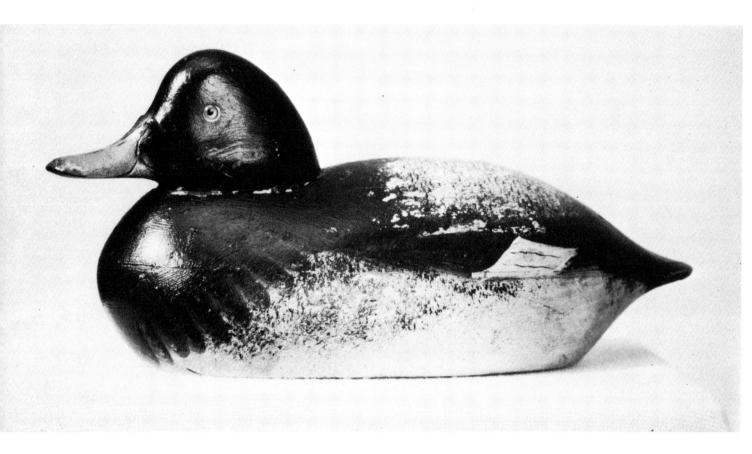

Mason Premier Grade Lowhead Blue Bill Drake

Mason Premier Grade Low-Head Blue Bill Hen

Mason Lowhead Challenge Blue Bill Drake

Mason Lowhead Premier Red Head Drake

Pair of Lowhead Challenge Blue Bills, two-thirds size

Mason Lowhead Challenge Grade Red Head Hen

Mason Special Order Hen Canvas Back   Mason Special Order Red Head Drake

119

Harvey A. Stevens - the founder of the Stevens
Decoy Factory. 1840–1894

Stevens ad from 1886 <u>Forest and Stream</u>.

Stevens Decoy Factory

Some of the earliest and most stylish factory decoys are those made by the Stevens Decoy Factory. The clean, pure lines and exceptional paint style could qualify Stevens decoys as entrants in a sculpture competition. No extraneous details distract your eye. This very simplicity left the carver no room for error. In this case, less is more.

Stevens Decoy Factory is a bit of a misnomer. We classify Stevens with other factory products, even though they were completely hand-carved rather than lathe-turned. Because the decoys were nationally advertised in sporting journals and because their carving provided full-time employment, its commercial nature places it in the factory decoy category.

Production of these beautiful decoys was limited by the very nature of the hand-crafting operation. Hundreds of wooden ducks were made as opposed to the thousands manufactured by the other factories. Finding a Stevens decoy in original condition should be a challenge, but a worthy one!

Harvey A. Stevens, founder of the Stevens Decoy Factory, began his operation in a small shed in Weedsport, New York. Born in 1847, Harvey made his first blocks for his personal use. H. A. Stevens was reputed on somewhat dubious authority to have been a part-time hunting guide and market-gunner. He did live on the fringe of the Montezuma Swamp, a haven for migrating wildfowl, now a National Wildlife Refuge. Thus, ideal gunning was easily available to him and his brothers. His rig decoyed so well that local hunters requested some of Stevens' decoys for themselves. Harvey increased his output to meet this demand.

Encouraged by his success locally, he set his sights on selling his decoys nationwide. No exact date is known for the beginning of this business venture, although his first national advertising appeared in an 1880 "Forest and Stream" magazine. Soon H. A. was shipping his handiwork to hunters across the country.

Business prospered and the shed was bursting at the seams, so the brothers moved to a larger shop on the outskirts of Weedsport some time in the 1880's. Never a very large business, there were only eight employees at the all-time high. Two of Harvey's brothers, George and Fred, helped in the making of the decoys. George played a major part in the business, specializing in the carving, while it has been assumed that Fred assisted in painting the decoys.

Harvey Stevens "manufactured" decoys in this location until his death in 1894. George and Fred continued production for several years, using Harvey's templates to carve the birds. The exact date when George Stevens put away the tools and the paintbrushes for the last time is not known, but then, exact dates and decoys don't seem to go together. Dates and numbers seem very unimportant. What we appreciate is the finished product - its style and beauty.

Stevens Red Head Drake Round Bottom Style.

Extremely Rare Stevens Widgeon Drake

Exceedingly Rare Stevens Wood Duck Hen

Stevens Blue Bill Drake (Round Bottom Style)

Stevens Black Duck

Stevens Blue Wing Teal Drake, Sitting on an
original bag from the factory

H. A. Stevens' "horse" vise, used in carving the decoys.

Stevens Red Head Hen - round-bottom style

Stevens Blue Bill (Scaup) Hen and Drake (hump-back style)

Stevens Goldeneye Drake (hump-back style)

Dodge Pintail Drake

Peterson Blue Bill Drake

Pair of Peterson Green Wing Teal, Drake's bill restored

126

Dodge Hooded Merganser

Pair of Dodge Greenwing Teal

Dodge Eskimo Curlew

Identification of Stevens Decoys

Because Stevens decoys have such a distinctive style, they are relatively easy to identify. The problem is finding one!

The Stevens' used templates or patterns in their carving. A hatchet was used to rough-cut the body and it was then refined with a chisel, draw shave and rasp. A "horse" vise held the body securely while the carving was in progress. The templates and the "horse" vise are currently on display at the Shelburne Museum in Vermont.

Stevens used the best available white or yellow cedar because of its lightness and durability. The cedar fragrance must have filled their small shed. George Thompson, an avid Stevens collector, has seen evidence, both in painted and stripped Stevens decoys, where knots were removed and checks filled with white putty. This indicates that the well-cured cedar may not have been too plentiful around Weedsport and may also be testimony to a certain frugality, necessitiated by the stringent economy imposed by the home-operated business.

Harvey A. Stevens proudly states in his sales literature that "in painting, nothing but the best paint is used; and for style and neatness they are unsurpassed." He was justifiably proud of his product. The paint proved very durable as many decoys found are in good original paint. The artist's touch is clearly evident in Stevens' work. Much time and effort was spent on the painting. He clearly tried to duplicate the coloring of ducks in their natural state.

The Stevens Decoy Factory made three styles of decoys: round-bottom, flat-bottom, and "intermediate" styles have been found.

The most frequently found Stevens decoys are the round-bottom style which was manufactured later than the flat-bottom. H. A. Stevens changed to this style early in the 1880's because of superior ability to ride in water.

Stevens Mallard Drake and Hen (round-bottom style)

Stevens Bufflehead Drake (round-bottom style)

Stevens Red Head Drake (hump-back style)

These decoys were made from two pieces of cedar - head and body. The wide, oval body was solid with a paddle-like tail. The paddle-like style is the most often seen, but also bearing the stencilled imprint of George (G. W.) Stevens, a number of "flare-type" tails were made - i.e. with the tail tapering to a gently curved point at the tip end. It is believed that these may have been experimental. Very few have come to light over the years. George Thompson has two - one a pintail drake, the other a widgeon drake. He has also seen one green wing teal of similar construction. A wooden dowel ran through the head and neck and into the body. Glass eyes from Germany were used to simulate the color of the wild duck eyes.

There were two 7/8" holes drilled in the bottom. The front hole had a recessed staple to hold the anchor line; the rear hole was filled with melted lead. Occasionally more than one hole filled with the leaded weight will be found. This was probably done to enable it to ride better in rough water.

Upon completion, the decoy was placed in a drawstring canvas bag for protection, then boxed by the dozen and shipped.

The earliest style is the flat-bottom or "humpback." It was also a two-piece decoy with a solid body. Some of these early "humpback" models lack the two 7/8" holes in the bottom and they were usually unsigned. Although the flat-bottom style was replaced by the round bottom-style, Harvey Stevens did continue to make some "humpbacks" through the 1890's. Of the two styles, the round-bottom is much more common than the flat-bottom.

There was a period when Stevens made a decoy quite unlike the early flat-bottomed "humpback" and by no means as refined as the later round-bottomed. It has been generally assumed for years that these rather crude decoys, known to collectors as "intermediates" or "goiter-necks," evolved from experimentation with the "humpback's" style and represent a stage of transition from the earlier to the later style. These blocks are rarely found, and it is believed that their numbers are minimal, that the experimentation was short-lived. They had rounded sides and bottom, were comb-painted, and had rather high necks which could have been termed slightly grotesque because of the suggestion of a goiter or "Adam's apple." There may have been a variety of species, but the only ones seen were drake scaup.

Stevens Goldeneye Drake (round-bottom style)

As a link in the Stevens saga they are eminently collectible, but they are generally considered by far the least appealing examples of the brothers' work.

Although H. A. Stevens claims in his sales literature to have signed all decoys after 1891, many authentic Stevens have been found with no signature. The unusual style of a Stevens decoy is signature enough. Stevens' signed decoys were marked in one of several ways. 1) Some early flat-bottoms are stenciled H. A. STEVENS, MAKER, WEEDSPORT, N. Y.; 2) The stencil usually found on the later decoys is H. A. STEVENS, MAKER, WEEDSPORT, N. Y. STANDARD DECOYS. 3) Several were signed in pencil by H. A. in cursive. 4) George Stevens sometimes burned a brand in the bottom of his which said G. W. STEVENS, WEEDSPORT, N. Y. Examples are also found which bear the printed stencil, as well as the brand. 5) A western N. Y. collector owns a matched pair of "intermediate" scaup, each with a small paper label glued to the underside of the bill and is imprinted with the Stevens Company name! This obviously indicates that at one point in time such a method of identification was used. While owning a Stevens with a signature on the bottom is certainly a plus, the absence of one is not important in the authentication of the decoy.

Then, as now, people were willing to pay more for a product of superior quality. At ten dollars a dozen in 1891, H. A. Stevens <u>had</u> to have an excellent product in order to compete with the machine-turned decoys on the market. The Stevens Decoy Factory has passed into history, yet the enjoyment and appreciation of their superb artistry continues to grow. What a wonderful legacy to leave!

Stevens Red Head Hen and Drake (round-bottom style)

Rare Dodge Gadwalls, Drake and Hen

Pair of Dodge Mallards, Drake and Hen

Peterson and Dodge Decoy Factories

Detroit Duo

George Peterson & Jasper N. Dodge

      Decoy collectors, being a very accepting lot, seem unconcerned with the scarcity of hard facts about many decoy makers. It's a good thing because the Peterson - Dodge jigsaw puzzle has numerous pieces missing. How many decoys were made? How did these men become interested in decoy making? How many helpers did they have? The list of un-answered questions goes on. Luckily, some pieces have recently turned up, thanks to the research of Bernard W. Crandell, helping us to complete the puzzle.

Dodge Black Duck in mint condition

Dodge Blue Bill Hen

Although George Peterson and Jasper Dodge were NOT in business together, their relationship makes it hard to treat them separately. They were two of the earliest manufacturers of factory decoys, whose work continues to bring enjoyment today.

While Peterson and Dodge decoys don't create quite the excitement that Mason, the other famous Detroit maker does, they are an important part of the factory decoy picture. Being predecessors to Mason, it would be interesting to know what effect, if any, Peterson and Dodge had on Mason's style.

George Peterson

George Peterson, forerunner to both Dodge and Mason, first set up his decoy business in 1873 at 68 and 70 Fort Street East, Detroit, Michigan. As a manufacturer of duck decoys, Peterson drew from his past experience as a chair maker, saw maker, carpenter and a machinist. Talented with his hands, he applied this knowledge in carving his stylish birds. His first shop, located on the second floor of the Mellus Saw Factory, was shared

Peterson Canvas Back Drake

with William Whitehall, a "wood turner." Hoping to make his business a success, he placed an advertisement in the December 6, 1873 issue of "The American Sportsman." I wonder how many customers that brought in?

Peterson relocated his shop in 1875, moving to 278 Division Street, Detroit. Frank Lambert, a painter, helped Peterson with the decoy business and became a partner a year or two before the business was sold to Jasper Dodge in 1884.

The exact number of decoys manufactured by George Peterson is not known, but the small size of his operation and the short length of time he was in business most likely limited his decoy production.

Of the two makers, Peterson's decoys have more aesthetic appeal than most Dodges. A lighter touch is evident in the body and head style and the painting is more artistically done. George Peterson definitely had a feel for the wood.

There are some characteristics commonly found on Peterson decoys. They had a sloped, pronounced breast and a sleek, thinnish body similar to Standard Grade Masons. The bodies were lathe-turned; both solid and hollow body decoys were made, the solid body being more common. Carving between the head and the bill and carving as separation of the mandibles is present on Petersons. Brush swirls in the primer coat of paint are found, although they're not as prominent as those found on Masons. Peterson used scalloped breast painting on some of his decoys, a technique copied by Dodge and Mason. Put these all together and you have a fine, early decoy. A welcome addition to any collection!

Jasper N. Dodge

In 1884, Jasper Dodge bought the decoy business from George Peterson, expanding the small one he had started in his home in 1883. Previously a salesman and clerk, Dodge decided to try his hand at decoy manufacturing at the age of 55.

Although the location of Dodge's shop was the same as Petersons, the similarity ends there. Jasper Dodge's style was quite different - or his styles would be a better term.

Dodge ad from 1886 Forest and Stream

J. N. DODGE,
276 & 278 Division Street,
DETROIT, MICH.

The only manufacturer of White Cedar Decoy Ducks. Cedar is the lightest and most durable wood. Also Geese, Brant, Swan, Coot, Snipe and Plover Decoys. All decoys made larger than the natural bird, and a perfect imitation. Illustrated price list free.

Dodge Canvas Back Drake

Dodge Barrow's Goldeneye Drake

Because Dodge advertised he would copy any decoy sent to him at no extra charge, the variety of styles is rather disconcerting. Hunters must have availed themselves of this option when you consider the range of quality and style. This makes identification of some Dodge decoys difficult but challenging!

There are some common factors to consider when identifying Dodges. All bodies were made of white cedar and were lathe-turned. He offered both solid and hollow models, the large majority were solid. Most bodies have high, wide shoulders and a blunt tail, giving the decoys a heavier look than the other factory birds. The head had carving between the head and bill, but rarely had carving to separate the mandibles, as did Peterson. Dodge used glass, tack, and painted eyes in his decoys.

The thin primer coat of paint reveals no swirls, but some Dodges do have scalloped breast paint and feathering. While many Dodge decoys have great eye appeal - a folky charm, others indicate the utilitarian use for which they were intended.

Jasper Dodge manufactured a full line of decoys - ducks, geese, swans, coot, brant, snipe, and plovers. In addition, he sold duck and turkey calls, plus the made-to-order models. He must have been a very busy man. For ten years, Dodge decoys were shipped all over the country. The demand for his products dwindled greatly, the exact reasons are only speculation, so in 1894 the Dodge Decoy Factory closed its doors.

At age 65, Dodge was not ready to retire to a rocking chair, so instead he turned to oar manufacturing. He became President of the Detroit Canoe and Oar Works from 1905—1908. Jasper Dodge finally retired to Bay City, Michigan, where he died in 1909 at the age of 80.

The emergence of the folk art market has been one factor in making these decoys of Peterson and Dodge so desirable. The desire to hold on to our past is strong. We own them because we appreciate their charm and style, and they also remind of a time long past.

Dodge Canada Goose

Decoys As An Investment

The inflation spiral shoots upward like a rocket. Gold and silver prices are on a roller coaster ride. Stocks and bonds offer little stability, while interest on savings accounts can't keep pace with inflation. What can the average person, who has a little money or a lot to invest, do to get a decent return on his investment? Although we never started collecting decoys solely for investment, we found it is a fun way to make the most of our money. We certainly don't recommend liquidating your assets and rushing out to buy decoys, but if decoys do appeal to you, it can be very rewarding. The plus to decoys is you have them around to enjoy in your home or office, not gathering dust in a safety deposit box. They still gather dust but that's a small price to pay.

Folk art, generally considered to be those objects made by persons with little or no formal training in that craft, has gained steadily in popularity during the last decade, as well as in value. People are looking backward, searching for a piece of the past to preserve, and decoys are a part of this heritage. In a December 19, 1979 Time article on "Art and Auctions," duck decoys were listed as one of the "well-crafted objects becoming ever scarcer, and soaring in value."

Lucky are those who had been collecting decoys before it became fashionable. Their initial investment has grown appreciably in the last ten years. Those of you just beginning your collection - there's no time like today.

There is one small catch to the whole thing and one you should consider. You wouldn't think you could become attached to a "piece of wood," but they worm their way into your heart. We, like other collectors, have certain decoys which we wouldn't sell if they were foreclosing on the house. So you do have to sell before you can make any money. Seems most collectors sell and then turn around and buy a better decoy. A vicious cycle, but you have a heck of a time doing it! At least you know, if you get the willpower to sell, you'll make a tidy profit.

Before You Buy

It's practically impossible to pick up a magazine or antiques periodical and not find decoys as featured props in the advertisements or as subjects in articles on antique auctions and shows.

There are two essential points to keep in mind before you embark on your mission. 1) Buy the very best decoy you can afford. 2) Learn all there is to know about the decoys that appeal to you the most.

It is much wiser to buy one very good decoy than five mediocre ones. Quality decoys will increase in value, while the best use for some decoys is as firewood. Decide which makers appeal to you and then concentrate on getting the most quality for your money. This pays off later if you decide to trade or sell your collection. You'll always find a buyer for fine quality birds, but a poorly crafted one is hard to give away.

What To Look For

Once you decide to take the plunge, many factors need to be considered when buying a decoy. Condition, style, rarity, maker, price, special significance, and most importantly, personal appeal. Study your potential purchase carefully.

Condition

When studying a decoy, examine it carefully to determine the condition of the paint and body. As a rule, the better the condition, the more it will cost. If you're not a purist, a decoy with some imperfections is perfectly acceptable and very collectible.

First, check the paint to see if it is original and not repainted. As decorating accessories, repainted decoys are fine - if they are priced accordingly, but even famous maker birds lose a lot of value if not in original paint. Some feel it's better to have a repainted rare example than none at all, but that's up to the individual.

You learn to recognize original paint by studying original paint decoys. Study photographs carefully and personally handle as many as possible. Most knowledgable collectors can help point out what to look for. They are often an excellent source of information.

Look in the cracks and crevices, look around the neck and around the eyes. There should not be any paint inside age cracks or paint where neck filler is missing. Overpaint can sometimes be removed to reveal the original paint, although traces of paint usually remain. A "taken-down" decoy can be a welcome addition to your collection but the price and value should be lower than one in 100% original paint.

Secondly, check the condition of the head and body. Many of the decoys you find show signs of use. Part of the bill may be missing, the tail may be chipped, or there may be an age crack. Remember - most of the birds were working decoys and the hunters certainly had no idea they were using "folk art" of the future. Signs of wear received in the line of duty honestly reflect its original use. They impart a sense of character sometimes missing in in mint condition decoy. You can easily imagine them bobbing on the water, luring unsuspecting ducks to their final resting place.

Style

Style - that overall excellence that sets some decoys above the rest - is largely a matter of individual taste. Certain decoys attract your attention while others leave you cold. The same bird you're enraptured with might not interest another collector in the least.

Each geographical region's decoys have certain characteristics germane to that area. Ducks from the Connecticut area by Ben Holmes or "Shang" Wheeler bear little resemblance to those from the Illinois River area by Bert Graves or Robert Elliston.

Decoys from the same area often bear a great similarity to each other because a style popular in their vicinity was imitated by others. Also, the water conditions over which the ducks were hunted would have been comparable.

Look for decoys whose style pleases you. Many have an eclectic collection with many decoys by different makers, while others concentrate on ones from a certain location or a particular maker. Do what is right for you.

Whatever you decide, choose decoys with pleasing lines - a well-shaped head and body are essential! The decoy's sculptural merits should be the first thing to consider. If it looks like it was carved in the dark with a hatchet, no amount of original paint is going to help! Finer details, like feather and bill carving, are assests but the lack of these certainly does not detract from the duck. Many collectors prefer the smooth, simple lines. It's purely personal preference. With the variety of decoy styles available, finding one you like should be easy.

Price

Decoy prices change so swiftly and depend on so many different factors that we will make no attempt to give price ranges for decoys. We feel these prices tell nothing about

YOUR decoy and with values spiraling upward, the figures are out-dated before the book is published. Also, the price depends largely on how much the collector wants a particular bird. If he wants a special decoy, especially a rarer species, he may pay more than it is really worth to have it in his collection. Pricing is a real sticky wicket so what can you do to find out?

One of the best ways to check prices is to attend any local decoy shows in your area. Lots of buying, selling, and trading goes on. (And you thought fishermen had tall tales to tell. You ain't heard nothing 'til you hear some of the sad stories of the duck that got away.) You can check prices on the birds for sale to get an idea. Some collectors even will do appraisals; they usually have a sign on their table.

The shows are a good way for beginning collectors to meet others from your locale who can show you their ducks and share their knowledge. Like proud parents, decoy collectors can't wait to show off the latest member of the "family"! We've spent many pleasurable hours talking about decoys and admiring a friend's favorites. We learned a lot in the process. As a result, wonderful friendships were formed. This, more than anything, is a good reason to rush right out to the nearest show.

Many collectors and dealers send out lists of ducks for sale or trade. A good periodical for those interested in buying is the North American Decoy Trader. It's full of ads listing ones for sale and trade and it will enable you to start corresponding with other collectors, especially if you can't get to shows.

Periodicals on antiques such as Maine Antique Digest, The Magazine Antiques, Ohio Antiques Review, Antiques & The Arts Weekly, and others occasionally have articles on decoys and the prices they bring. The advertisers feature them in many ads and the articles on different antique shows list prices fairly frequently. They make for interesting reading!

Prices in auction catalogs can be misleading to the beginner. People get caught up in the fever of bidding and sometimes pay more for a decoy at an auction than they might pay for the same decoy bought from a dealer or private collector. Before you start bidding, set a top price and stick to it. We all like to have the winning bid, but be sure you know its value. This way you won't get stuck. Auctions are lots of fun and a good place to find decoys. Just bring your better judgement with you.

Also remember that auction prices don't take the commission paid to the auction house into consideration. The seller pays and now the buyer in many auction houses pays a commission also. This tends to give a inflated price to many decoys. On the other hand, sometimes auction prices are lower than expected. You might read an article and say, "Why wasn't I there!!! It's so cheap." What isn't noted is that the bill was replaced or the entire duck was repainted. This is not done intentionally because the writers can't be expected to be experts in every field. It's sometimes hard for "experts" to tell. It just points out that while it's good to know what kind of prices they are bringing on the auction block, take the prices with a grain of salt.

With Mason decoys, usually the higher the grade, the more expensive the decoy. A Premier Mallard will usually cost much more than a Standard Grade Mallard in the same condition. Condition and rarity do make for exceptions. A Premier Grade in poor condition might be the same as a Standard Grade in mint condition. A Glass Eye Green Wing in excellent condition would be more valuable than a Premier Blue Bill in excellent shape due to its rarity. It's the old story of supply and demand.

I guess the best advice of all is to find a person you can trust and let them help you build a good collection. This way you might avoid any pitfalls along the way. Have fun!

Special Significance

Some decoys are considered "special" by some because it was owned by a well-known collector, it was used by a certain gunning club, or it was on display or in a book. This title is not always dependent on superior quality. It doesn't necessarily make the decoy more valuable but it certainly doesn't hurt.

If a well-known collector like William Mackey had a decoy in his personal collection, most people assume it must be a top quality duck. They might pick it over a decoy of equal quality because of his name on the bottom. Gunning clubs were popular during the period most decoys were made. The St. Clair Flats Gunning Club, for instance, had a rig of wonderful decoys. Owning one of these ducks reminds you of a special time in history and the men who made it history. Because the quality of decoys in exhibits and in books is usually very good, they also are desirable.

None of these things may mean a thing to you or maybe they will. If nothing else, it makes collecting an interesting hobby!

Restoration and Care

Decoys were made for the hunter, not the collector, so inevitably many ducks show signs of wear. Picked up by the head, carelessly placed in a boat or bag, and then put out on the water. Since the best hunting is usually during the worst weather, rough water would bang them around. Cold, wet, and exhausted, the last thing a hunter was worried about is chipping the paint on his decoy. It's a wonder they look as good as they do! For these reasons, decoys sometimes need a little help to make them look their best. Purists prefer to leave the battle scars, while others like to treat their bird to a facelift. Most collectors do feel legitimate restoration lowers the value, but it remains a very collectible decoy.

Some common restorations are replacement of a tail chip, replacement of all or part of a bill, replacement of eyes, and removal of overpaint. Tails and bills were prone to

142

damage because of the hard treatment they got during hunting season. Eyes were broken or fell out over a period of time. Decoys were repainted when the original paint got worn. Sometimes a duck in beautiful original paint was repainted because the hunter needed another species. So if you want your decoys to look letter perfect, do have them restored.

Being made from wood, decoys dry out over a period of time. We found that treating ours with a commercial turpentine and beeswax mixture helps to bring out the color of the paint and nourishes the wood. We've used it on our wood furniture for years and no permanent finish is left.

If you find a duck that is very dirty, wash it first with mild soap and water. Try a test spot first, although the original paint of a decoy designed for use on the water shouldn't wash off. We've found there are a few things to avoid. Linseed oil darkens the wood and holds dirt. Over a period of time you'll have a grungy decoy. Varnish also darkens the wood and will yellow eventually. NEVER, I repeat, NEVER put a coat of polyurethene on any decoy. It gives a plastic look to the duck and it is practically impossible to get off! No self-respecting collector will buy one with it on the decoy. Try to stay away from anything that changes the finish permanently.

Whether you are a purist or a restorer, or somewhere in between, enjoy your collection and take your clues from the individual decoy.

Mason, Stevens, and Dodge factory decoys and related accessories

Rarity

All Mason collectors dream of finding a Mason Spoon Bill, rarest of the rare. We always want what's least obtainable and this is true of decoys. Certain species are less common than others for several reasons.

Buffleheads and Ruddy Ducks were too small to bother with and weren't widely hunted. Few decoys were needed and few are found. Eiders, Old Squaws, Scoters, and Mergansers are all sea ducks and were only hunted regionally. Even on the East Coast where they are found, their fishy taste made them unpopular as table food, so many were not required.

Many ducks such as Blue Bills decoyed only to their own species so they are found in great numbers, while Wood Ducks would decoy to almost anything. Why bother to carve them if they weren't necessary?

Rarity also depends upon the maker and the area in which he lived. For example, a Bert Graves Black Duck would be considered rare while a Mallard would not. This is because few Black Ducks were found in his flyway, so there would be little reason to carve one; Mallards were hunted extensively in his area so many were needed for a rig.

A wider range of species was offered by the various factories because they were trying to meet hunting needs on a national rather than a regional level.

Rare decoys have an added plus. They're usually more valuable than commonly found blocks. Exclusivity does have its advantages.

Maker

If you put two decoys of equal quality on a table, one carved anonymously and the other by a famous maker, the majority would choose the one by the well-known maker. Collectors feel it would be a safer investment and they have an idea of its future value.

Famous makers are just that for a reason. The quality of the workmanship is generally superior to others in the area. Skilled in painting and carving, they utilized these talents when making their product. Because of their superior quality, the value is greater initially and at resale. This does not mean that every decoy by a well-known maker is valuable by virtue of a name. It must be judged on its sculptural merits alone.

This doesn't mean you have to limit yourself to famous maker birds. Numerous "no name" blocks deserve a place on your shelf. It's good to have a good mix of both.

Where to Find Decoys

Half of the fun of collecting is tracking down the leads you get. Actually purchasing the decoy is anticlimatic sometimes. Here are loads of places to look but no guarantee you'll find any.

Decoy shows, as previously mentioned, are a sure bet. With tables full of decoys you should find something to strike your fancy. There is a beautiful calender available at many of the shows that gives the location, date, and person to contact for the major shows and auctions.

Auctions feature more and more decoys all the time. It's a good way to spend a day - even if you don't buy a thing. The Richard Bourne Auction in Hyannis, Massachusetts is well-known for the quality ducks put on the block each summer. The prestigious auction galleries in New York City - Sotheby Park-Bernet, Phillips, Christies, and Doyle - often have excellent decoys. Don't forget the local auctions which are usually listed in the newspaper and in antique periodicals.

Antique shops and shows carry more and more decoys all the time. You can also find gunning accessories like gun powder cans, hunting prints, shotgun shells, duck calls, etc., to complement your collection. We got started this way. Besides, it's fun to poke around in all those old things.

Some great finds have turned up at flea markets and garage sales. What is junk to them may be the steal of a lifetime.

Private collectors and dealers are excellent sources. The barter system is alive and well and practiced by collectors all over the country.

Enlist your friends and relatives in your search. You never know what will turn up on your doorstep. Frank Klay, the photographer who took all the outstanding outdoor shots and many of the black and white photos, stopped by for a photographic session. There was a peculiar glint in his eyes and a "have I got a surprise for you" smile on his face. He casually mentioned he'd been out looking for decoys the day before and here's what he had found. Taking a cardboard box out of the car, we proceeded to unwrap each one.

They had been kept out in his friend's barn and he was kind enough to let them be photographed. There on the ground were these beauties. A pair of Premier Blue Bills, a pair of Challenge Goldeneyes, a pair of Challenge Mergansers, two Black-Bellied Plovers, and a two piece Curlew. We almost had a massive coronary right there in the front yard!! Every one of them was in original paint and excellent condition. Unfortunately, anonymous doesn't want to part with them. Can you blame him? Just in case he changes his mind, I'll clear a little shelf space.

A gathering of Mason shore birds.

Collage in oil of Mason Decoys.

Drawings - Finer Points To Look For In Mason Decoys

Masons At A Glance

Once you know which features to look for on each grade, distinguishing a Challenge Grade from a Standard Grade is quite easy. The drawings incorporate the identifying features of each grade and can be used as a guide. Some decoys will have all the details while others will only have a few. It is very important to know which feature is a MUST for that grade and species, and which is a MAYBE. Used in conjunction with the color photographs, you should have little trouble classifying Mason decoys.

Try to learn the general body and head shape of the different species, both hen and drake. The Pintail and the Merganser have a distinctive shape, but others look similar to each other. You then must study the details, such as bill carving and type of eye, to place a decoy.

Once you've seen several Masons, you'll be surprised at the ease with which you can pronounce it a Tack Eye Mallard Drake with absolute certainty.

Premier Grade

Premier Masons are easily identified by the notched bill carving and the carved nail at the end of the bill. Swirls should be evident in the paint, although scalloped breast paint swirls are only on certain species. With few exceptions, Premier bodies are hollow, plump, and well-formed. All have glass eyes and the finer details, such as feathering, are usually present.

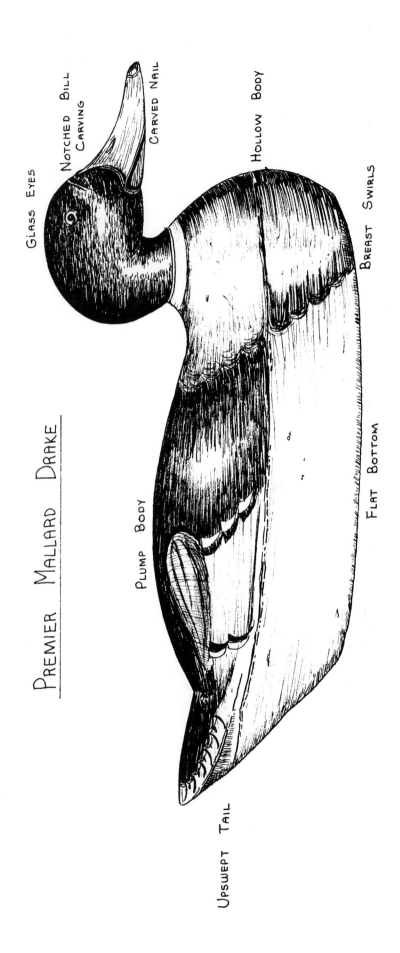

Premier Mallard Drake

GLASS EYES

NOTCHED BILL CARVING

CARVED NAIL

HOLLOW BODY

BREAST SWIRLS

PLUMP BODY

FLAT BOTTOM

UPSWEPT TAIL

PREMIER MALLARD DRAKE

Premier Mallard Hen

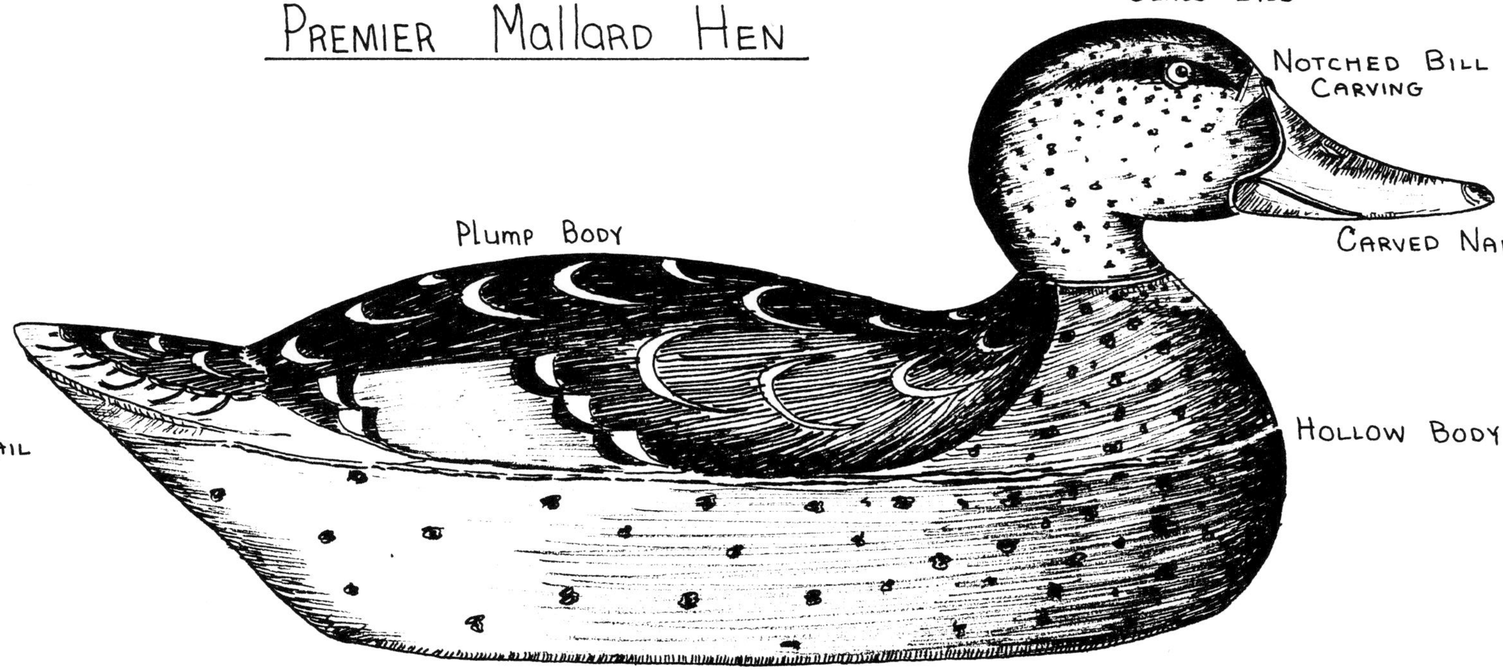

Glass Eyes

Notched Bill Carving

Carved Nail

Hollow Body

Plump Body

Upswept Tail

Flat Bottom

149

Challenge Grade

Challenge Grade Masons all have carving between the head and bill and between the mandibles. Glass eyes are found in all species and painting details are normally present. The majority have solid bodies, although some hollow-bodied Challenge Masons are found. The body size is slightly smaller than the Premier Grade in all dimensions. Look for the swirling in the base paint.

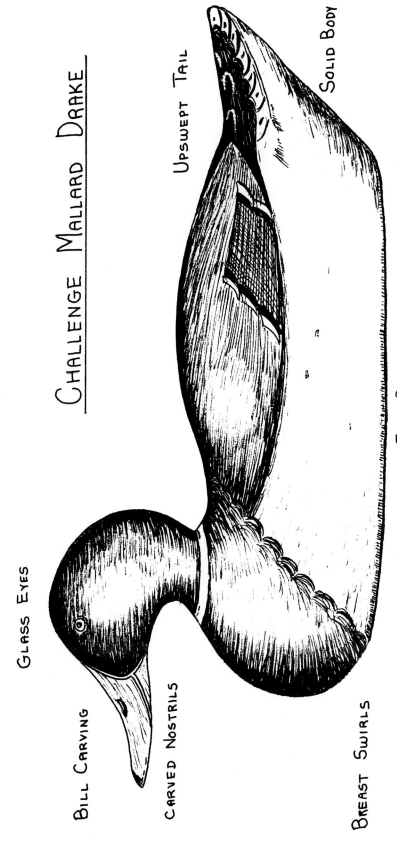

CHALLENGE MALLARD DRAKE

UPSWEPT TAIL

SOLID BODY

GLASS EYES

BILL CARVING

CARVED NOSTRILS

FLAT BOTTOM

BREAST SWIRLS

CHALLENGE GRADE MALLARD DRAKE

Challenge Mallard Hen

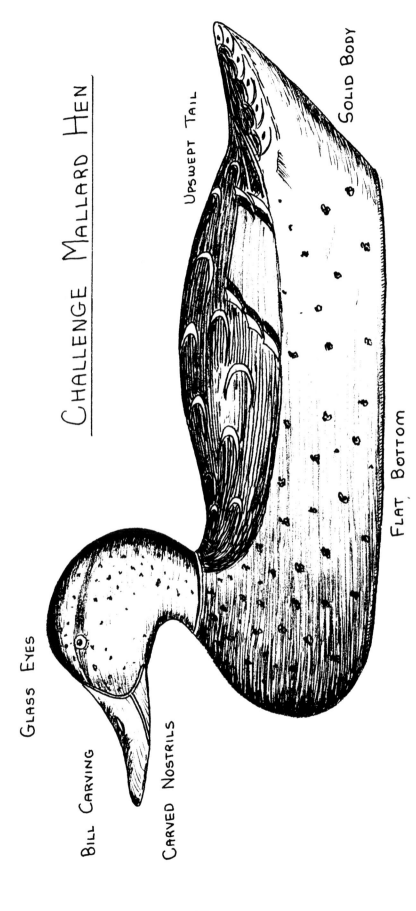

Glass Eyes

Bill Carving

Carved Nostrils

Upswept Tail

Solid Body

Flat Bottom

Challenge Grade Mallard Hen

151

No. 1 - Glass Eye

All Glass Eye or "Detroit" Grade Masons have glass eyes, no bill carving, and a solid body. Most species have a flatter tail and smaller body than the Premier or Challenge Grades. Neck filler was used to join the head and body though it is not always found intact.

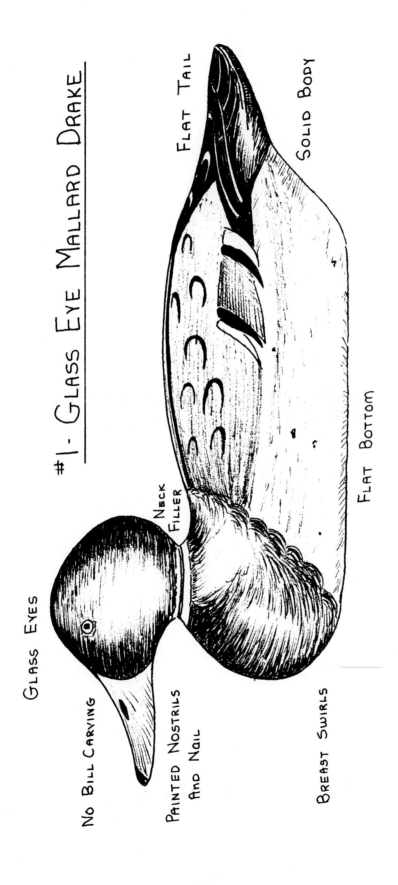

#1 - GLASS EYE MALLARD DRAKE

GLASS EYES

NO BILL CARVING

PAINTED NOSTRILS
AND NAIL

NECK
FILLER

FLAT TAIL

SOLID BODY

FLAT BOTTOM

BREAST SWIRLS

#1. MALLARD DRAKE

#1- Glass Eye Mallard Hen

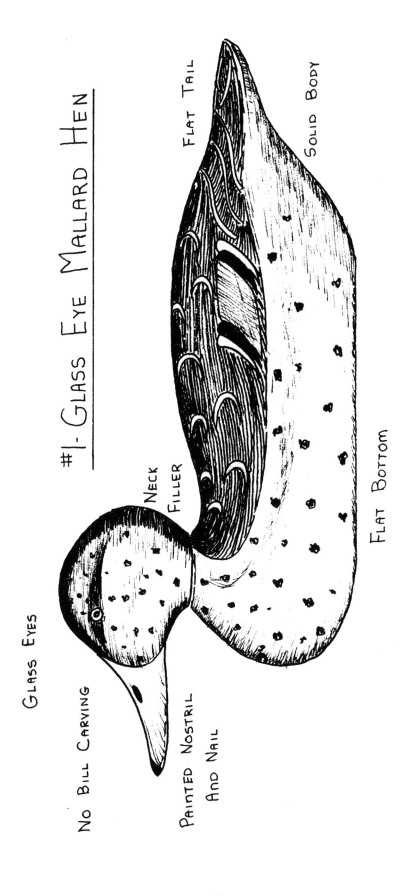

Flat Tail

Solid Body

Neck Filler

Flat Bottom

Glass Eyes

No Bill Carving

Painted Nostril And Nail

#1. MALLARD HEN

153

No. 2 - Tack Eye

Mason used metal tacks for eyes on this grade. The solid body is the same size as the Glass Eye but lacks some of the detailed painting found on that grade. On those species with breast paint, it is defined by a straight line rather than scallops. Neck filler was used around the neck.

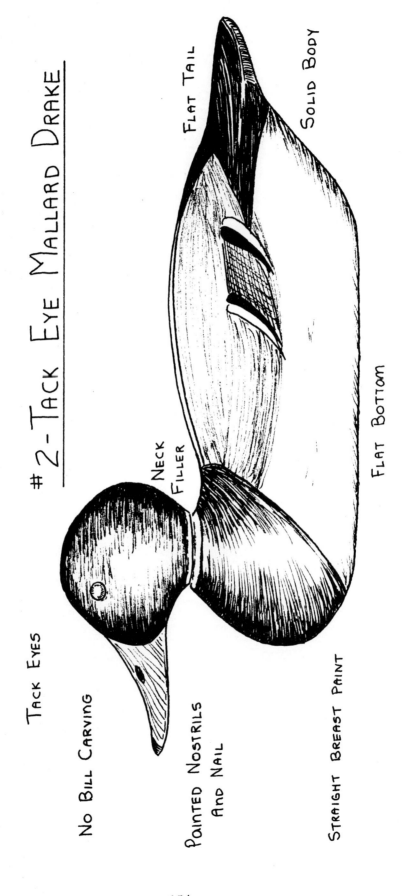

#2-Tack Eye Mallard Drake

Flat Tail

Solid Body

Neck Filler

Tack Eyes

No Bill Carving

Painted Nostrils And Nail

Flat Bottom

Straight Breast Paint

#2 Mallard Drake

154

#2-Tack Eye Mallard Hen

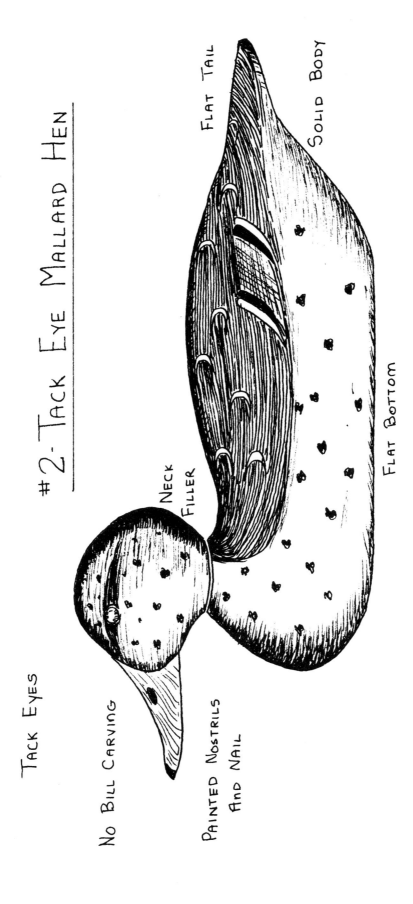

Flat Tail

Solid Body

Neck Filler

Flat Bottom

Tack Eyes

No Bill Carving

Painted Nostrils And Nail

#2 Mallard Hen

No. 3 - Painted Eye

No. 3 Masons all have an orangish painted eye with a black center. Some Painted Eyes have had tacks or glass eyes added but the orange eye is still evident. The tube-like is narrower than the Glass Eye and Tack Eye and the painting details are generally missing. Neck filler was used to fill in around the neck and body.

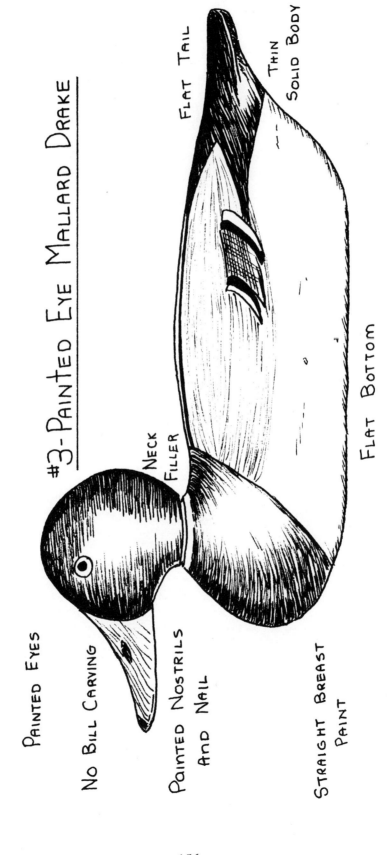

#3 - Painted Eye Mallard Drake

Flat Tail

Thin Solid Body

Painted Eyes

No Bill Carving

Painted Nostrils And Nail

Neck Filler

Straight Breast Paint

Flat Bottom

#3 Mallard Drake

#3- Painted Eye Mallard Hen

Painted Eyes

No Bill Carving

Painted Nostrils
And Nail

Neck
Filler

Flat Tail

Thin
Solid Body

Flat Bottom

#3 Mallard Hen

157

Bibliography

Bourne, Richard. "Bourne Decoy Auction" catalogs. 1967–1980

Cheever, Byron. *Mason Decoys.* Hillcrest Publications, 1974.

Cheever, Byron. *North American Decoys Magazine.* Hillcrest Publications, 1971–1979.

Colio, Quintina. *American Decoys.* Science Press, 1972.

Earnest, Adele. *The Art of the Decoy.* Clarkson N. Potter, 1965. Reissued, Bramhall House.

Egan, Mrs. Raymond. *Toller Trader Magazine.* Cazenovia, New York, (December, 1968).

Mackey, William. *American Bird Decoys.* Dutton, 1965. Reissued, Schiffer Publishing Limited, 1979.

Parmalee, Paul W. and Loomis, Forrest D. *Decoys and Decoy Carvers of Illinois.* Northern Illinois University Press, 1969.

Sorenson, Harold D. *Decoy Collector's Guide.* Harold Sorenson, Publisher, 1963–1979.

Starr, George Ross, Jr. *Decoys of the Atlantic Flyway.* Winchester Press, 1974.

Walsh, Harry. *The Outlaw Gunner.* Tidewater Publications, 1971.

Webster, David and Kehoe, William. *Decoys At Shelburne Museum.* Shelburne Museum, 1961, 1971.

Suggested Reading

Cheever, Byron. *Mason Decoys.* Hillcrest Publications, 1974.

Cheever, Byron, ed. *North American Decoys Magazine.* Hillcrest Publications, 1972–1979.

Colio, Quintina. *American Decoys.* Science Press, 1972.

Earnest, Adele. *The Art of the Decoy: American Bird Carvings.* Clarkson N. Potter, 1965. Reissued Bramhall House.

Fleckenstein, Henry. *Decoys of the Mid-Atlantic Region.* Schiffer Publications Limited, 1979.

Johnsgard, Paul A., ed. *The Bird Decoy.* University of Nebraska Press, 1976.

Mackey, William. *American Bird Decoys.* Dutton, 1965. Reissued Schiffer Publications Limited, 1979.

Murphy, Stanley. *Martha's Vineyard Decoys.* David R. Godine, 1978.

Parmalee and Loomis. *Decoys and Decoy Carvers of Illinois.* Northern Illinois University Press, 1969.

Reed, M. Clarke, ed. *Decoy World.* Quarterly periodical.

Sorenson, Harold D. *Decoy Collector's Guide.* Harold A. Sorenson, Publisher, 1963–1979.

Starr, George Ross, Jr. *Decoys of the Atlantic Flyway.* Winchester Press, 1974.

Webster, David and Kehoe, William. *Decoys at Shelburne Museum.* Shelburne Museum, 1961, 1971.

PERIODICALS

Antiques & The Arts Weekly. The Newtown Bee, Newtown, Conn., 06470

Bourne Auction Catalogues. Richard A. Bourne, Co., Inc., Hyannis, Mass., 02647

Magazine Antiques, The. 551 Fifth Avenue, New York, New York, 10017

Maine Antiques Digest. Jefferson Street, Waldoboro, Maine, 04572

North American Decoys Trader. Hillcrest Publications, Spanish Fork, Utah, 84660

Ohio Antiques Review. Worthington, Ohio, 43085

List of Plates

166

Index

K

Knot, *see Jacksnipe*
Kurkowske, William, 11, 12

L

Lambert, Frank, 135
Late style Mason, 29
Lesser scaup, *see Blue Bill*
Lowheads, 37, 113, 115, 117, 118
Magazine Antiques, The, 141
Maine Antiques Digest, 141
Mallard decoys, 25, 27, 69, 70, 71,
    72, 73, 74, 75, 128, 132
Market hunters, *vii, viii,* 49, 52, 88
Mason catalog, 12, 13, 14, 15, 16,
    17, 18, 19, 20, 21, 22, 23, 24
Mason Decoy factory, *viii,* 11, 12,
    134
Mason grades of decoys, 25, 26, 27,
    28, 29
Mason paint, 12, 25, 26, 27
Mason, Fred, 12
Mason, Herbert, 11, 12
Mason, Hugh, 12
Mason, William, 11, 12
Merganser decoys, 11, 27, 76, 77,
    78, 79, 127
Mud hen, 60

N

North American Decoys, 11
North American Decoys Trader,
    141

O

Ohio Antiques Review, 141
Old Squaw decoys, 80, 82, 113
Oversize Mason decoys, 54, 113

P

Painted Eye characteristics, 25, 29,
    156, 157
Painted Eye Mason decoys, 26, 35,
    43, 52, 59, 68, 71, 86, 91, 98
Peterson characteristics, 135
Peterson decoys; Blue Bill, 126;
    Canvas Back, 134; Green Wing
    Teal, 126
Peterson, George, *viii,* 133, 134,
    135, 138
Pintail decoys, 83, 84, 85, 86, 87,
    126, 130
Premier Grade characteristics, 12,
    25, 26, 148, 149
Premier Grade Masons, 26, 30, 34,
    39, 42, 45, 46, 49, 53, 54, 55,
    56, 57, 58, 67, 73, 74, 75, 78,
    82, 85, 86, 87, 90, 93, 94, 95,
    97, 98, 101, 102, 103
Premier stamp, 27

R

Red Head decoys, 88, 89, 90, 91,
    92, 113, 118, 119, 122, 124,
    129, 131
Rinshed, Fred, 12
Rinshed-Mason Company, 12
Robinsnipe, 107, 109, 111

S

Salesmen's samples, 113
Scoter, 60, 63
Seneca Lake, New York, 52
Seneca Lake Canvas Backs, 52, 55,
    56
Shelburne Museum, 100, 128
Sheldrake, *see Merganser*
Shorebirds, 107, 108, 109, 110,
    111, 112, 113, 114, 116, 127,
    145
Sinkbox, 88
Sleepers, *see Lowheads*
Snaky head, 27, 36, 53, 69
Special Order Masons, 42, 113,
    115, 119
Sprig, *see Pintail*
Standard Grade Mason decoys, 12,
    25, 28, 29
Stevens characteristics, 128, 130,
    132
Stevens decoys, Black duck, 123;
    Blue Bill, 123, 125, 130; Buffle-
    head, 129; Goldeneye, 125,
    130; Mallard, 128; Red Head,
    122, 124, 129, 131; Teal Blue
    Wing, 123, Green Wing, 130;
    Widgeon, 122; Wood Duck, 122
Stevens Decoy factory, *viii,* 120,
    121, 128, 130, 132
Stevens, Fred, 121
Stevens, George, 121, 130
Stevens, Harvey, A., 120, 121, 128,
    130, 132
Stevens stencil, 132
Stevens' styles of decoys; flat-
    bottom, 128, 130; Humpback,
    125, 129; Round-bottom, 122,
    123, 124, 129, 130, 131
Stippling, 25, 27, 29
St. Clair Flats, 11, 12
Swan, 44, 49

T

Tack Eye characteristics, 28, 29,
    154, 155
Tack Eye Mason decoys, 33, 36,
    41, 57, 78, 84, 92, 94, 95, 103
Teal, Blue Wing, 93, 94, 95, 96, 97,
    98, 99, 123
Teal, Green Wing, 93, 95, 98, 126,
    127
Templates, 121, 128
Thompson, George, 128, 130

W

Weedsport, New York, *viii,* 121,
    128, 132
Whistler, *see Goldeneye*
Whitehall, William, 135
Widgeon, 100, 101, 102, 103, 104,
    122
Willet decoys, 107, 108, 112, 114
Wood Duck decoys, 105, 106, 113,
    122

Y

Yellowlegs decoys, 107, 108, 114

168